# delicious.
# baking

**CAKES · TARTS · PIES · PUDDINGS · BISCUITS**

eye
to
eye
media

# welcome.

"COME ALONG inside… We'll see if tea and BUNS can make the world a better place." Those words from *The Wind in the Willows* sum up the POWER OF BAKING. Somehow the melding of good things in the heat of the oven, releasing the scents of BUTTER, sugar, spice, maybe a grating of lemon, maybe CHOCOLATE – definitely chocolate – is the promise of good times. It's a one-stop fix linked to childhood memories. It means COSINESS; it means warmth. Cakes are made to share, not to have one SLICE cut out and be hidden away in a tin.

My view is, with baking, the SIMPLEST RECIPES are often the best – a straightforward marriage of ingredients in harmony. This special baking collection, brought to you from the experts in the DELICIOUS. magazine kitchens, has every cake and bake recipe you could need, from BROWNIES to cupcakes to savoury pies and lemon cake. Every recipe is thoroughly TESTED so you can be confident your cake will rise to the occasion – and, most importantly, TASTE good.

If you have only half an hour and need a rapid homemade fix of SWEETNESS, try the double choc-chip cookies on p14. If you have longer and are up for a challenge, try the MACAROONS on p10. If you want savoury comfort food, it's sounding like PIE – try the Chinese-spiced beef on p96. Whenever the need to bake strikes, whatever your whim, there's a recipe here to satisfy. HAPPY BAKING…

**KAREN BARNES** EDITOR,
DELICIOUS. MAGAZINE

Eye to Eye Media
Axe & Bottle Court
70 Newcomen Street
London SE1 1YT
eyetoeyemedia.co.uk

First published by Eye to Eye Media Ltd 2012

© Eye to Eye Media Ltd

A catalogue record of this book is available from the British Library

ISBN 978-0-9573598-0-2

Printed and bound in the UK by Ancient House Press

# contents.

Strawberry ricciarelli, p9

# biscuits and cookies

Pistachio biscuits, p9

Almond puffs

## almond puffs

**Makes 24**

140g blanched almonds, lightly toasted
115g unsalted butter, softened
2 tbsp caster sugar
½ tsp vanilla extract
150g plain flour
1 tbsp icing sugar

1. Preheat the oven to 180°C/fan160°C/
gas 4 and line a baking tray with baking
paper. Put the almonds in a food
processor and whizz until finely ground.
2. Beat the butter and caster sugar
together in a bowl using an electric
hand mixer until pale and fluffy. Add the
ground almonds and vanilla, then sift in
the flour. Beat the mixture until you
have a smooth dough.
3. Use your hands to roll the dough into
walnut-size balls. Put on the lined tray,
spaced 2cm apart, and bake for 20-25
minutes until golden.
4. Sift the icing sugar over the biscuits
and return to the oven for 2 minutes
more. Leave to cool on the tray. Store
for 2-3 days in an airtight container.

## pistachio biscuits

**Makes 20**

130g shelled, unsalted pistachios
50g plain flour
165g caster sugar
3 medium free-range egg whites
Icing sugar to dust

1. Preheat the oven to 180°C/fan160°C/
gas 4 and line 2 baking trays with baking
paper. Whizz three-quarters of the
pistachios in a food processor until finely
ground, tip into a bowl, then stir in the
flour and 110g of the caster sugar. Chop
the remaining nuts into slivers.
2. In another bowl, whisk the egg whites
with an electric hand mixer until soft
peaks form. Add the rest of the caster
sugar and beat until stiff and glossy,
then fold into the pistachio mixture.
3. Space heaped tablespoons of the
batter 2cm apart on the lined trays and
sprinkle with slivers of pistachio.
4. Bake for 12-15 minutes until golden.
Leave to cool for 5 minutes on the trays,
then transfer to a wire rack to cool
completely. Dust with icing sugar.

## strawberry ricciarelli

**Makes 15**

These traditional Italian biscuits from
Tuscany are perfect with dessert wine.

300g blanched almonds
Grated zest of 1 small orange
200g caster sugar
2 medium free-range egg whites
100g strawberries, hulled and chopped
Icing sugar to dust

1. Preheat the oven to 160°C/fan140°C/
gas 3. Line 2 baking trays with baking
paper. Put the almonds on a baking tray
and toast in the oven for 4-5 minutes until
lightly golden. Allow to cool completely.
2. Whizz the almonds and orange
zest in a food processor until coarsely
ground. Stir in half the caster sugar.
3. Use an electric hand mixer to whisk
the egg whites to firm peaks, then
gradually add the remaining 100g caster
sugar and beat until smooth and glossy.
Fold the nut mixture and the chopped
strawberries into the meringue.
4. Using 2 dessertspoons, shape
the mixture into ovals and put on the
prepared trays, spaced 3cm apart.
5. Dust with icing sugar and bake for
12-15 minutes until lightly golden but still
soft in the centre. Cool on the trays for
5 minutes, then transfer to a wire rack
to cool completely. Dust with icing sugar.

**biscuits and cookies.**

Peanut butter cookies

## peanut butter cookies
### Makes 18-20

125g unsalted butter, softened
170g crunchy peanut butter
110g caster sugar
1 medium free-range egg
260g plain flour
½ tsp baking powder
50g unsalted roasted peanuts,
finely chopped
Cinnamon sugar to dust

1. Preheat the oven to 180°C/fan160°C/
gas 4 and line 2 baking trays with
baking paper.

2. Beat the butter, peanut butter and
sugar in the bowl of a stand mixer
for 5 minutes until light and creamy.
3. Add the egg and beat to combine. Sift
the flour, baking powder and a pinch of
salt into a bowl. Add this to the butter
mixture and beat until just combined.
4. Put the chopped nuts on a plate. Roll
heaped tablespoons of dough into balls,
press the tops into the nuts and flatten
slightly. Put on baking trays, 4cm apart.
5. Bake for 12-15 minutes until golden
and cooked through. Cool on the trays
for 5 minutes, then transfer to a wire
rack to cool completely. Dust with
cinnamon sugar to serve.

## macaroons
### Makes 20
This recipe makes vanilla macaroons. To
make chocolate ones, replace 2 tbsp of
the icing sugar with 2 tbsp cocoa powder
and omit the vanilla extract. In the filling,
use 3-4 tbsp Baileys in place of the cocoa.

175g icing sugar
125g ground almonds
3 medium free-range egg whites, at
room temperature
75g caster sugar
1 tsp vanilla extract

FOR THE FILLING
150g unsalted butter, softened
80g icing sugar, sifted
2 tbsp cocoa powder, sifted

1. Preheat the oven to 160°C/fan140°C/
gas 3. Line 2 baking trays with baking
paper. Put the icing sugar and ground
almonds in a food processor and pulse
until well combined. Sift into a bowl.
2. In the bowl of a stand mixer, whisk
the egg whites with a pinch of salt until
soft peaks form, then whisk in the
caster sugar, 1 tbsp at a time, until the
mixture is thick and glossy. Whisk in
the vanilla extract until combined.
3. Fold half the almond mixture into
the egg whites. Add the rest, then use
a spatula to beat it for 3-5 minutes until
the mixture is smooth and shiny, and
has a ribbon-like consistency as it falls
from the spatula. Spoon into a piping
bag fitted with a plain 1cm nozzle.
4. Pipe 40 x 3cm rounds on to the baking
trays, slightly spaced out. Leave to dry at
room temperature for 10-15 minutes
(you should be able to touch them lightly
without any mixture sticking to your
finger). Bake for 15 minutes until dry
on top. Allow to cool completely.
5. To make the filling, beat the butter
in the bowl of a stand mixer until light
and fluffy, then beat in the icing sugar
and the cocoa.
6. Spread this thinly over the flat sides of
half the macaroons, then sandwich them
together with the remaining macaroons.

Vanilla and chocolate macaroons

Hazelnut and orange biscotti

Mocha meringues

## hazelnut and orange biscotti

**Makes about 40**

220g caster sugar
2 medium free-range eggs
Finely grated zest of 1 lemon
Finely grated zest of 1 orange
300g plain flour, sifted, plus extra
for sprinkling
½ tsp baking powder
100g blanched hazelnuts, toasted
Icing sugar to dust

1. Preheat the oven to 170°C/fan150°C/
gas 3½. Line a large baking tray with
baking paper.
2. Put the sugar, eggs and all the citrus
zest in a large bowl, then beat with an
electric hand mixer until fluffy and pale.
3. Fold in the sifted flour, baking powder
and hazelnuts, then use your hands to
lightly knead the dough on a floured
work surface until smooth.
4. Divide the mixture in half. Form
2 logs about 25cm x 5cm and put
on the prepared baking tray, leaving
a little space between them. Bake
for 20-25 minutes until the dough is
firm to the touch and lightly golden.
Allow to cool completely on the tray
(this will take about an hour).
5. Preheat the oven to 140°C/fan120°C/
gas 1. Once the dough is cool, use
a small serrated knife to cut each log
diagonally into 1cm-thick slices. Return
the biscotti to the oven for 20-25
minutes, turning once, until completely
dry. Leave to cool on the tray.
6. Store the biscotti in an airtight
container for 2-3 weeks. Dust with icing
sugar when ready to serve.

## mocha meringues

**Makes 30**

1 tbsp cocoa powder, sifted
3 tsp instant coffee granules
3 medium free-range egg whites
175g caster sugar
½ tsp vanilla extract
75g good-quality dark chocolate,
chopped

1. Preheat the oven to 140°C/fan120°C/
gas 1. Line 2 large baking trays with
baking paper.
2. Put the cocoa and 2 tsp coffee
granules in a food processor or spice
grinder and pulse until finely ground.
3. Put the egg whites in the bowl of an
electric mixer and whisk to soft peaks.
Continuing to whisk, slowly add the
caster sugar, 1 tbsp at a time, until you
have a stiff, glossy meringue. Whisk in
the vanilla extract and the coffee-cocoa
powder. Spoon the mixture into a piping
bag fitted with a plain 1cm nozzle.
4. Pipe 60 x 3cm meringues on to the
baking trays, spacing them 2cm apart.
Bake for 45 minutes or until dry and
golden on the surface. Remove from the
oven and cool for 5 minutes on the trays.
5. Meanwhile, to make the filling, put
the chocolate and remaining 1 tsp coffee
granules in a bowl set over a pan of
simmering water (making sure the bowl
doesn't touch the water) and heat,
stirring, until the chocolate has melted.
Allow to cool slightly before use.
6. Spread 1 tsp chocolate on the flat side
of half the meringues and sandwich
them together with the remaining
meringues. Set aside for an hour for the
chocolate to set before serving.

# biscuits and cookies.

Orange drops

## orange drops

**Makes 24**

These cute little biscuits, fragrant with orange zest, are perfect with an afternoon cup of tea. You can make the dough a day ahead and chill overnight wrapped in cling film, then bring back to room temperature before using.

225g plain flour
½ tsp baking powder
40g ground almonds
90g salted butter, at room temperature
110g caster sugar
Grated zest of 1 orange
1 tsp vanilla extract
2 medium free-range eggs
Icing sugar to dust

1. Preheat the oven to 180°C/fan160°C/gas 4 and line 2 baking trays with baking paper.

2. Combine the flour and baking powder in a bowl, then stir in the ground almonds. In a separate bowl, beat the butter and sugar with an electric hand mixer until thick and pale. Beat in the zest, vanilla and 1 egg, then stir this into the flour mixture until well combined.

3. Divide the dough into 24 pieces, then roll each into a ball. Put one on the work surface and pinch it twice to form a peak. Transfer to the trays, then repeat with the rest of the dough. Beat the remaining egg with 1 tbsp water, then use to lightly glaze the biscuits.

4. Bake for 10-12 minutes until the biscuits are firm but still pale. (Rotate the trays halfway through cooking, if necessary, to ensure even baking.) Leave to cool on the trays for 5 minutes, then transfer to a wire rack to cool completely. Dust with icing sugar. Store in an airtight container for up to 5 days.

## double choc-chip cookies

**Makes 16**

125g unsalted butter, softened
250g soft dark brown sugar
1 tsp vanilla extract
1 free-range egg
225g plain flour
½ tsp baking powder
100g good-quality dark chocolate, roughly chopped
100g good-quality white chocolate, roughly chopped

1. Preheat the oven to 180°C/fan160°C/gas 4. Line a baking tray with baking paper.

2. Put the butter and sugar in a bowl and beat with an electric hand mixer until pale and fluffy. Add the vanilla extract and egg, then continue to beat until just combined. Sift in the flour, baking powder and a pinch of salt, then fold to combine. Stir through the chunks of dark and white chocolate.

3. Put heaped tablespoons of the mixture 4-5cm apart on the tray. Bake for 15-20 minutes until golden. Remove from the oven and allow to cool for 5 minutes before transferring to a wire rack to cool completely. Store in an airtight container for 2-3 days.

Double choc-chip cookies

Easter biscuits

biscuits

Gluten-free nut biscuits

## easter biscuits

**Makes about 40**

450g plain flour
½ tsp ground cinnamon
¼ tsp ground nutmeg
225g salted butter, softened
220g caster sugar, plus 2 tbsp extra
to sprinkle
2 medium free-range eggs
110g currants
Finely grated zest of 1 lemon

1. Sift the flour and spices into a bowl. In another bowl, beat the butter and sugar with an electric hand mixer until fluffy and pale, then add the eggs, one at a time, beating well after each addition. Fold in the flour mixture, then, once combined, stir in the currants and zest. Shape into a disc, wrap in cling film and chill for at least 2 hours.
2. Preheat the oven to 180°C/fan160°C/gas 4. Line 3 baking trays with sheets of baking paper.
3. Divide the dough into 4. Roll out each into a 5mm-thick round (keeping the remaining dough covered and chilled), and cut out biscuits using a fluted 6cm round cutter. Put on the trays, spaced 2cm apart. Repeat with the remaining dough, re-rolling the trimmings to make 40 biscuits. Chill for 15 minutes.
4. Sprinkle the biscuits with extra sugar and bake for 10 minutes or until firm to the touch, but still pale. Cool the biscuits on the tray for 5 minutes, then transfer to a rack to cool completely. Keep in an airtight container for up to 3 days.

## gluten-free nut biscuits

**Makes about 24**

You could substitute 185g chopped chocolate for the fruit and nuts. Rice flour can be found in the free-from section of many supermarkets.

125g unsalted butter, softened
125g soft light brown sugar
1 large free-range egg, lightly beaten
1 tsp vanilla extract
2 tbsp natural yogurt
150g rice flour
150g unsalted mixed nuts and dried fruit, roughly chopped

1. Preheat the oven to 180°C/fan160°C/gas 4. Line 2 baking trays with sheets of baking paper.
2. Using an electric hand mixer, beat the butter and sugar together in a bowl until fluffy and pale.
3. Add the egg and vanilla, then beat until combined. Fold in the yogurt, rice flour and chopped fruit and nut mix.
4. Put slightly rounded tablespoons of the mixture onto trays, flatten, then bake for 12 minutes or until golden. Cool on trays for 5 minutes, then move to a wire rack to cool completely. Store in an airtight container for up to 3 days.

Banana bread with
passion fruit butter, p21

# sweet and savoury breads

Plaited fruit loaf, p21

Sour cherry and
marzipan stollen

## sour cherry and marzipan stollen
**Makes 1 loaf**

100g butter, softened, plus extra
to grease
300g strong white bread flour, plus
extra to dust
¼ tsp salt
55g caster sugar
7g sachet fast-action dried yeast
Finely grated zest of 1 orange
100g dried sour cherries
80g almonds, roughly chopped
150ml milk, warmed
125g good-quality marzipan

**FOR THE ICING**
100g icing sugar, sifted
30ml orange juice

1. Grease a large baking tray. Sift the flour and salt into a large bowl. Rub in the butter with your fingers to give fine crumbs. Stir in the sugar, yeast, zest, cherries and chopped nuts. Make a well in the centre, then gradually pour in the milk, mixing until you have a soft dough.
2. Turn out on to a floured surface and knead for 10 minutes or until the dough is shiny and elastic. Put in a lightly oiled bowl and cover with cling film. Leave in a warm place for about 1 hour or until the dough has doubled in size.
3. Knock back the dough with your fist and roll out on a lightly floured surface into a rectangle about 20cm x 10cm.
4. Roll the marzipan into a sausage slightly shorter than the dough and put it lengthways in the middle of the dough. Fold the sides over to enclose the marzipan and press together to seal. Put the dough on the baking tray, seam-side down, and loosely cover with greased cling film. Leave to rise for 30 minutes.
5. Preheat the oven to 160°C/fan140°C/gas 3. Mix the icing sugar and orange juice together until smooth and runny.
6. Bake the stollen for 50 minutes until it's golden and the base sounds hollow when tapped. Transfer to a wire rack and cool completely. Spread the icing over and leave to set. Slice to serve.

## plaited fruit loaf
**Makes 2 loaves**

120g butter
80ml milk
75g caster sugar
400g plain flour, plus extra to dust
7g sachet fast-action dried yeast
3 medium free-range eggs, beaten
125g chopped glacé apricots or cherries
55g mixed peel
Oil or butter to grease
1-2 tbsp flaked almonds

1. Melt the butter with the milk and sugar over a low heat, stirring to dissolve the sugar. Leave to cool to lukewarm.
2. Put the flour and yeast in a stand mixer fitted with a dough hook and whizz to combine. Add the milk mixture and beaten eggs, reserving 1 tbsp egg to glaze, then beat for 5-10 minutes until you have a soft, elastic dough.
3. Turn out on to a floured surface. Shape into a rough rectangle, 1cm thick. Scatter with a quarter each of the glacé fruit and peel, then fold the sides into the centre so they overlap like a letter. Flatten slightly with a rolling pin, then repeat until all the fruit and peel are incorporated.
4. Knead for 1-2 minutes to evenly distribute the fruit, then roll into a ball and put in a lightly oiled bowl. Cover with a lightly oiled piece of cling film and leave in a warm place for 1 hour or until the dough has doubled in size.
5. Line a baking tray with baking paper. Put the dough on a floured surface. Divide into 6 pieces and roll each into a strand, about 35cm long and 2.5cm wide, slightly tapering at the ends. Lay 3 strands side by side on the baking sheet, with a small space between each, and plait by bringing the right strand over the one next to it, then the left one over the one next to it and so on, tucking the ends underneath. Repeat with the remaining strands. Cover and leave for 1 hour or until almost doubled in size.
6. Preheat the oven to 180°C/fan160°C/gas 4. Brush with egg and sprinkle with the almonds. Bake for 25-30 minutes until lightly golden. Cool on a wire rack.

## banana bread with passion fruit butter
**Makes 1 loaf**

Oil or butter to grease
250g plain flour
1½ tsp baking powder
75g caster sugar
80g soft light brown sugar
1 tsp ground cinnamon
2 medium free-range eggs, beaten
1 tsp vanilla extract
3 overripe bananas, mashed

**FOR THE PASSION FRUIT BUTTER**
250g cream cheese, softened
100g good-quality lemon curd
40g icing sugar, sifted
Pulp of 4 passion fruit

1. Preheat the oven to 160°C/fan140°C/gas 3. Grease a 20cm x 10cm loaf tin and line it with baking paper. Sift the flour and baking powder into a large bowl, then stir in both sugars and the cinnamon. Add the beaten eggs, vanilla extract and mashed banana, then stir until well combined. Spoon into the prepared tin.
2. Bake for 45-50 minutes until a skewer inserted in the centre comes out clean. Cool in the tin for 10 minutes, then turn out on to a wire rack to cool completely.
3. Meanwhile, to make the butter, put the cream cheese, lemon curd and sugar in a food processor and pulse briefly until just combined (don't overwork the mixture, or it'll be too runny). Add the passion fruit pulp and pulse 2-3 times to combine, then chill until ready to serve. (Passion fruit butter will keep in a sealed container for up to a week in the fridge.) Thickly slice the banana bread and serve with the passion fruit butter.

21

**sweet and savoury breads.**

Cranberry loaf

## cranberry loaf
**Makes 1 large loaf**

60g butter, melted, plus
extra to grease
500g plain flour
220g caster sugar
1 tbsp baking powder
1 tsp salt
2 medium free-range eggs, beaten
350ml milk
200g frozen cranberries, thawed
and roughly chopped
95g mixed dried fruit
100g hazelnuts, toasted and
roughly chopped

**FOR THE CRANBERRY SAUCE**
200g fresh or frozen cranberries
110g caster sugar
Juice of 4 small oranges
1 vanilla pod, split and seeds scraped

1. Preheat the oven to 180°C/fan160°C/
gas 4. Grease an 8cm deep, 25cm x
10cm loaf tin and line the base with
baking paper.
2. Sift the flour, 220g caster sugar, the
baking powder and salt into a large
bowl. Beat the eggs, milk and butter
together in a separate bowl, then fold
them into the dry ingredients, followed
by the cranberries, dried fruit and nuts.
3. Spoon the mixture into the tin, then
bake for 55 minutes or until a skewer
pushed into the centre comes out clean.
Cool in the tin for 10 minutes, then turn
out on to a wire rack to cool completely.
4. To make the sauce, put all the
ingredients in a saucepan over a medium
heat. Cook, stirring occasionally, for 6-8
minutes until the fruit breaks down and
the mixture thickens. Set aside to cool.
5. Serve the loaf with cranberry sauce
and butter or cream cheese.

## saffron spice loaf
**Makes 1 loaf**

1 tbsp butter, softened, plus
extra to grease
125ml milk, plus extra if needed
1-2 pinches of saffron threads
60ml double cream, plus extra to serve
325g strong white bread flour, plus
extra to dust
¼ tsp salt
7g sachet fast-action dried yeast
1 tbsp caster sugar
½ tsp mixed spice
25g sultanas
25g raisins
1 tbsp honey

1. Grease a 20cm x 10cm loaf tin. Gently
heat the milk in a small pan to just
below boiling point. Stir in the saffron
threads, take the pan off the heat and
leave to infuse for 15 minutes.
2. Add the cream to the milk and heat
gently for 2 minutes (don't let it boil),
then take off the heat and cool slightly.
3. Meanwhile, sift the flour and salt into
a bowl. Stir in the yeast, sugar and
mixed spice. Make a well in the centre
and add the warm milk. Mix to form a
soft dough, adding extra milk if needed.
4. Turn out on to a floured surface and
knead for 15 minutes, gradually adding
the butter and dried fruit, until the
dough is soft and elastic. Transfer
to a lightly greased bowl and cover
with cling film. Leave in a warm place
for 1 hour or until doubled in size.
5. Knock back the dough, then knead
on a floured surface for 5 minutes.
Divide into 3 pieces and roll each into
a strand slightly longer than the tin.
Plait the strands together and tuck the
ends underneath as you put the plait
in the prepared tin. Cover with greased
cling film and leave in a warm place for
1½ hours or until doubled in size.
6. Preheat the oven to 180°C/fan160°C/
gas 4. Bake for 25 minutes or until well
risen and golden. Brush with honey and
leave to cool in the tin for 5-10 minutes,
then turn out on to a wire rack to cool
completely. Serve with whipped cream.

Saffron spice loaf

Feta, tomato and rosemary
flowerpot breads

Olive and thyme focaccia

## feta, tomato and rosemary flowerpot breads

**Makes 8**

1 tbsp olive oil, plus extra to grease
500g strong white bread flour, plus extra to dust
240g sun-blush tomatoes in oil
1 tsp salt
2 tbsp finely chopped fresh rosemary leaves, plus 8 small sprigs
7g sachet fast-action dried yeast
250ml warm water
150g feta, crumbled, plus extra to scatter

1. Grease and flour 8 x 7cm terracotta pots or 8 holes in 2 large muffin tins.
2. Drain the tomatoes, reserving 1 tbsp of the oil and 8 tomatoes to garnish. Chop the remaining tomatoes.
3. Sift the flour and salt into a large bowl. Stir in the chopped rosemary and yeast. Make a well in the centre and gradually mix in the olive oil, chopped tomatoes and their reserved oil, together with the warm water, until the mixture comes together into a dough. Add a little more water if it seems too dry.
4. Knead the dough on a floured surface for 10 minutes, then knead in the feta. Shape into 8 balls and put in the prepared pots or tins. Set aside, loosely covered with a clean tea towel, in a warm spot for 30 minutes until doubled in size.
5. Preheat the oven to 220°C/fan200°C/gas 7. Top each ball with one of the reserved tomatoes, some extra feta and a sprig of rosemary. Bake for 25 minutes or until golden and cooked through, then serve warm with butter.

## olive and thyme focaccia

**Makes 1 loaf**

500g strong white bread flour, plus extra to dust
1 tsp sea salt, plus extra to sprinkle
2 tbsp fresh thyme leaves, plus extra to scatter
7g sachet fast-action dried yeast
2 tbsp olive oil, plus extra to grease and drizzle
250ml warm water
100g pitted black olives, chopped

1. Sift the flour and salt into a large bowl. Stir in the thyme and yeast. Gradually mix in the oil and water to make a dough.
2. Add a little more water if the dough seems too dry. Tip on to a lightly floured surface and knead for 5 minutes. Put in an oiled bowl, cover with a clean tea towel and leave in a warm place for 1½ hours or until doubled in size.
3. Knock back the dough and knead in the olives. Use your hands to shape it into a large circle and place on an oiled baking tray. Rest in a warm place for 45 minutes or until doubled in size.
4. Press your fingertips into the dough to make indents all over the surface, drizzle with extra oil, scatter with the extra sea salt and thyme, then bake for 25 minutes or until golden. Drizzle with a little more olive oil and serve warm.

Goat's cheese, olive
and potato bread

## chocolate and hazelnut panettone

**Makes 1 large loaf**

125g butter, softened, plus extra
to grease
350g strong white bread flour, plus
extra to dust
¼ tsp salt
7g sachet fast-action dried yeast
55g caster sugar
50g raisins
50g toasted hazelnuts, roughly chopped
Finely grated zest of 1 orange
3 medium free-range eggs, lightly
beaten
80ml milk, warmed, plus
extra if needed
50g good-quality dark chocolate (70%
cocoa solids), roughly chopped
Icing sugar to dust

1. Grease a fluted 22cm bundt tin
(available from wayfair.co.uk).
2. Sift the flour and salt into a large
bowl. Stir in the yeast, sugar, raisins,
chopped nuts and orange zest. Make
a well in the centre, then add the eggs,
milk and 100g of the butter. Mix well
until thoroughly combined.
3. Knead the mixture on a floured surface
for 10 minutes or until the dough is
smooth and elastic. Put in a lightly
greased bowl and cover with cling film.
Leave in a warm place for at least 1 hour
or until the dough has doubled in size.
4. Knock back the dough, then knead for
a further 5 minutes on a floured surface.
Knead in the chocolate, a little at a time,
but working as quickly as possible to
avoid it melting. Shape the dough into
a log and put in the tin, joining the ends
together. Cover and leave for another
30 minutes or until it has doubled
in size. Meanwhile preheat the oven
to 180°C/fan160°C/gas 4.
5. Melt the remaining 25g butter
and brush it over the dough. Bake for
30-35 minutes or until the loaf is golden
and a skewer inserted in the centre
comes out clean. Leave to cool
completely in the tin, then turn out
and dust with icing sugar to serve.

## goat's cheese, olive and potato bread

**Serves 6**

Oil or butter to grease
190g self-raising flour, plus
extra to dust
190g waxy potatoes, peeled
and grated
1 onion, grated
1 tbsp chopped fresh rosemary leaves,
plus an extra sprig to garnish
100g goat's cheese, crumbled
75g pitted kalamata olives, chopped
1 medium free-range egg
1-2 tbsp milk
2 tsp wholegrain mustard

1. Preheat the oven to 200°C/fan180°C/
gas 6. Grease a baking tray and dust it
lightly with flour.
2. Sift the flour into a large bowl. Add
the potatoes and onion, season and stir.
Fold in the rosemary, 90g of the goat's
cheese and 60g of the olives. Beat the
egg, milk and mustard in a jug, then
pour this into the flour mixture.
3. Stir together to make a rough dough,
then put the dough on a well-floured
surface and shape into a round. Transfer
to the tray, dot with the rest of the cheese
and olives, then scatter with the extra
rosemary sprigs. Dust with flour and bake
for 45 minutes, until the base of the bread
sounds hollow when tapped. Serve warm.

Chocolate and hazelnut panettone

Cardamom-scented
chelsea buns

## cardamom-scented chelsea buns
**Makes 9 buns**

50g butter, chopped, plus 50g butter, softened, plus extra to grease
450g strong white flour, plus extra to dust
7g sachet fast-action dried yeast
30g caster sugar
1 medium free-range egg
165ml milk, warmed, plus extra if necessary
1 tsp cardamom seeds, lightly crushed
55g sultanas
50g currants
50g muscovado or brown sugar
2 tsp honey
2 tbsp unsalted shelled pistachios, chopped

1. Grease a deep 23cm square cake tin. Sift the flour and a pinch of salt into a large bowl. Rub in the chopped butter until it resembles fine crumbs. Stir in the yeast.
2. In a separate bowl, whisk together the sugar and egg. Add to the dry ingredients along with the milk. Mix it all together into a soft dough, adding a little more milk if it seems too dry.
3. Turn the dough out on to a lightly floured surface and knead for 15 minutes or until smooth and elastic. Put in a lightly greased bowl, cover with cling film and leave in a warm place to rise for about 1 hour or until doubled in size.
4. Knock back and roll out on a floured surface into a 25cm x 35cm rectangle.
5. Spread the softened butter over the dough, then scatter with the cardamom, dried fruit and sugar. Starting with one of the long sides, roll it up into a log, then trim off the ends.
6. Slice into 9 rounds and arrange in the tin, cut-side up, with the slices touching. Cover with lightly greased cling film and leave for 1 hour to double in size. Preheat the oven to 200°C/fan180°C/gas 6.
7. Bake for 25-30 minutes until golden. Brush with honey, then sprinkle with pistachios. Cool in the tin for 10 minutes, then move to a wire rack or serve warm.

Chocolate banana bread

## chocolate banana bread
**Makes 1 loaf**

150g butter, plus extra to grease
300g plain flour, plus extra to dust
170g brown sugar
2 medium free-range eggs
1 tsp bicarbonate of soda
150ml milk
3 overripe bananas, mashed
50g good-quality dark chocolate, roughly chopped
50g walnuts, chopped

1. Preheat the oven to 180°C/fan160°C/gas 4. Grease and flour a 25cm x 10cm loaf tin.
2. Using an electric hand mixer, beat the butter and sugar in a bowl until light and fluffy. Add the eggs, one at a time, beating well after each addition.
3. Sift in the flour, bicarbonate of soda and a pinch of salt. Beat well, then gradually add the milk.
4. Fold the mashed bananas into the mixture with the chopped chocolate and walnuts. Spoon into the loaf tin, then level the top with the back of a spoon.
5. Bake for 60-70 minutes or until a skewer pushed into the centre comes out clean (cover with foil if it starts to brown too quickly). Leave to cool in the tin for at least 15 minutes before turning out. Slice and serve warm.

Pineapple and chilli upside-down cake, p33

# cakes

Lemon polenta cake
with mascarpone and
lemon curd, p33

Chocolate mud cake

## chocolate mud cake

**Serves 16-18**

250g butter, chopped, plus
extra to grease
200g good-quality dark chocolate,
chopped
1 tbsp instant coffee granules
100ml milk
250g self-raising flour
40g cocoa powder
250g caster sugar
4 medium free-range eggs, beaten
1 tsp vanilla extract
150ml soured cream
1 quantity ganache (see Basics, p124)

1. Preheat the oven to 160°C/fan140°C/
gas 3. Grease and line a deep 23cm
loose-bottomed cake tin.
2. Put the chocolate, butter, coffee and
milk in a heatproof bowl set over a pan
of barely simmering water (don't let
the bowl touch the water) and stir until
smooth. Remove from the heat and
set aside to cool completely.
3. Sift the flour and cocoa powder into a
bowl, then add the caster sugar. Fold into
the chocolate mixture along with the
eggs, vanilla extract and soured cream.
4. Pour into the prepared tin and bake
for 60-70 minutes until a skewer pushed
into the centre comes out with some
moist crumbs sticking to it but no raw
batter. Leave to cool completely in the tin.
5. Remove from the tin and spread
ganache evenly all over the cake,
swirling it into patterns.

## lemon polenta cake with mascarpone and lemon curd

**Serves 10**

330g butter, softened, plus
extra to grease
130g fine polenta, plus extra to dust
400g caster sugar
4 medium free-range eggs
300g ground almonds
1½ tsp baking powder
1 tbsp plain flour
Grated zest of 4 lemons, plus juice of 3
2 tbsp limoncello liqueur (optional)

**FOR THE ICING**
150ml double cream, whipped
250g mascarpone
2 tbsp icing sugar, sifted
85g lemon curd
Toasted flaked almonds to decorate

1. Preheat the oven to 160°C/fan140°C/
gas 3. Grease a round 23cm springform
tin, base line with baking paper, grease
again, then dust with a little polenta.
2. Use a stand mixer to beat the butter
and 300g of the sugar together until thick
and pale. Add the eggs, one at a time,
beating well after each addition. Fold in
the almonds, polenta, baking powder
and flour. Add the lemon zest and the
juice of 2 of the lemons, then mix well.
3. Spoon into the tin and smooth the top
with a knife. Bake for 1¼ hours or until
a skewer inserted into the centre comes
out clean (cover loosely with foil if the
top starts to colour too quickly).
4. Meanwhile, make a syrup by heating
the remaining 100g sugar, lemon juice,
and limoncello (if using) in a small pan.
When the cake is ready, pierce the top all
over with a skewer. Spoon the syrup over
the warm cake and leave to cool in the
tin for 15 minutes, then carefully remove
from the tin and cool on a wire rack.
5. To make the icing, whisk the cream,
mascarpone and icing sugar until
smooth. Put the cake on a serving plate
and spread with icing. Drizzle with lemon
curd, swirling it into the icing with a
skewer, then top with toasted almonds.

## pineapple and chilli upside-down cake

**Serves 8-10**

Adding chilli to a cake might seem
strange, but it really complements
the sweet pineapple in this
gorgeous dessert.

225g butter, softened, plus extra
to grease
250g golden syrup
1 long red chilli, seeds removed,
finely chopped
Finely grated zest of 1 lime
440g pineapple rings in syrup
220g caster sugar
4 medium free-range eggs, beaten
225g self-raising flour, sifted

1. Preheat the oven to 180°C/fan160°C/
gas 4. Grease a round 23cm cake tin and
line with baking paper.
2. Put the golden syrup, chilli and lime
zest in a small saucepan over a low heat
and stir for 2 minutes until warm. Pour
half the syrup into the cake tin, tilting
the tin so the syrup covers the base
evenly, then arrange 7 pineapple rings in
a single layer across the base (reserve
the pineapple syrup).
3. Put the butter and sugar in a large
bowl and beat using an electric hand
mixer until pale and fluffy. Beat in the
eggs, one at a time, beating well after
each addition to incorporate. Fold in the
flour and enough of the pineapple syrup
(about 1-2 tbsp) to give the mixture
a smooth consistency.
4. Chop the remaining pineapple rings
and stir them into the mixture. Spoon
the batter into the tin and level the
surface with a palette knife.
5. Bake for 45 minutes or until golden
and a skewer pushed into the centre
comes out clean (cover with baking
paper if it's browning too quickly).
6. Cool in the tin for 10 minutes, then
carefully invert on to a large serving
plate. Warm the remaining chilli syrup
in a small pan over a low heat, then
pour it over the cake.
7. Slice and serve warm or at room
temperature with ice cream.

Poppy seed and lemon
cake with cream cheese icing

## poppy seed and lemon cake with cream cheese icing

**Serves 8**

1 unsprayed pale yellow rose
3 medium free-range eggs,
plus 1 egg white
175g caster sugar, plus extra to dust
175g butter, softened, plus extra
to grease
Finely grated zest of 2 large lemons
250g self-raising flour, sifted
50g poppy seeds
95g thick Greek-style yogurt

**FOR THE CREAM CHEESE ICING**
250g cream cheese, at
room temperature
1 tbsp caster sugar
2 tsp lemon juice
1 tbsp thick Greek-style yogurt

1. Carefully remove the petals from the rose, brush with egg white and dust with caster sugar. Shake off any excess and leave to dry for 2-3 hours until brittle.
2. Preheat the oven to 150°C/fan130°C/gas 2. Grease and line a 1 litre loaf tin.
3. Beat the butter and sugar with an electric hand mixer until pale and fluffy. Beat in the zest and eggs, one at a time, beating well after each addition, adding 1 tbsp flour with the second and the last egg. Sift over the remaining flour and fold in with the poppy seeds and yogurt.
4. Spoon into the prepared tin and bake for 1 hour 10 minutes or until a skewer inserted into the centre comes out clean. Cool for 10 minutes in the tin, then turn out and cool on a wire rack.
5. To make the icing, beat all the ingredients with a wooden spoon until fluffy. Spread thickly over the cake and scatter with crystallised rose petals.

## victoria sandwich
**Serves 8-10**

175g butter, softened, plus extra
to grease
175g caster sugar, plus extra
to sprinkle
3 large free-range eggs
175g self-raising flour
60ml milk
110g raspberry jam

1. Preheat the oven to 180°C/fan160°C/gas 4. Cut 2 x 18cm discs of baking paper. Grease 2 x 18cm sandwich tins, line the bases with the discs, then grease again.
2. Put the butter in a stand mixer with the caster sugar and beat them together until pale and fluffy.
3. Add the eggs one by one, beating well after each addition. Sift over the flour and gently fold in with a spatula or metal spoon until combined. Stir in just enough milk to give the mixture a smooth dropping consistency.
4. Divide the mixture evenly between the tins, using scales for accuracy. Bake in the centre of the oven for 20-25 minutes until the tops are golden and a skewer pushed into the centre of one cake comes out clean (leave the other untouched so the top is perfect). Leave to cool in the cake tins for 10 minutes, then turn out on to a wire rack covered with a clean cotton tea towel to prevent marking. Carefully turn the cakes over, removing the towel, then leave on the rack to cool completely.
5. Once the cakes are cool, put the pierced cake, bottom-side up, on a cake stand and spread with the raspberry jam. Top with the other cake and sprinkle with caster sugar to serve.

Victoria sandwich

Raspberry and lime heart cake

Classic cheesecake

## raspberry and lime heart cake

**Serves 8-10**

250g butter, softened, plus extra
to grease
310g plain flour, plus extra to dust
1½ tsp baking powder
280g caster sugar
3 medium free-range eggs
Finely grated zest and juice of 2 lemons
Finely grated zest and juice of 2 limes
140g thick Greek-style yogurt
125ml milk
250g raspberries
60g icing sugar to dust
Crème fraîche to serve (optional)

1. Preheat the oven to 170°C/fan150°C/
gas 3½. Grease a 20cm heart-shaped
cake tin and dust with flour, shaking off
any excess. Sift the flour and baking
powder into a bowl.
2. Beat the butter and caster sugar
in a stand mixer until thick and pale.
Add the eggs, one at a time, beating
well after each addition.
3. Stir in the flour and baking powder,
a little at a time, then add the lemon and
lime zest and juice, the yogurt and the
milk and mix into a smooth batter.
4. Pour the batter into the prepared
cake tin and spread it out evenly using
a spatula. Bake for 1 hour 10 minutes,
or until the cake is golden and a skewer
pushed into the centre comes out
clean. Remove from the oven and
leave to cool in the tin.
5. Remove the cake from the tin and
arrange the raspberries on top. Sift
over the icing sugar and serve with
crème fraîche if you like.

## classic cheesecake

**Serves 8**

125g butter, melted, plus extra to grease
400g chocolate digestive biscuits
1.5kg cream cheese, softened
4 medium free-range eggs, beaten,
plus 2 egg whites whisked to stiff peaks
220g caster sugar
1 tsp vanilla extract
300ml double cream, whipped
Icing sugar to dust

1. Preheat the oven to 160°C/fan140°C/
gas 3. Grease a 24cm round springform
cake tin and base line with baking paper.
Crush the biscuits, stir in the butter,
then press them into the base of the tin.
Bake for 10 minutes, then set aside.
2. Briefly whizz the cream cheese in a
food processor. Add the whole eggs in
4 batches, then the sugar and vanilla,
and whizz to combine. Put in a bowl
and fold in the egg whites in 2 stages.
3. Pour the mixture into the tin and bake
for 1 hour 10 minutes or until just set
with a slight wobble in the centre. Turn
the oven off, open the door slightly and
leave the cake to cool completely in the
oven. Cover and chill for at least 3 hours,
then top with whipped cream and dust
with icing sugar.

# cakes.

Spiced fruit cake

## courgette and pistachio spice cake with lime icing
**Serves 10-12**

85ml sunflower oil, plus extra to grease
220g caster sugar
3 medium free-range eggs
1 tsp vanilla extract
75g unsalted shelled pistachios, finely chopped
60g ground almonds
3 medium courgettes, grated and any excess liquid squeezed out
1 tsp ground cardamom
1 tsp ground mixed spice
½ tsp bicarbonate of soda
225g self-raising flour
75g plain flour

**FOR THE LIME ICING**
180g butter, softened
200g icing sugar, sifted
250g cream cheese, softened
Finely grated zest and juice of 1 lime
35g unsalted pistachios, chopped into slivers

1. Preheat the oven to 170°C/fan150°C/gas 3½. Grease a 22cm round springform cake tin and line the base and sides with baking paper.
2. Use an electric hand mixer to whisk the oil, sugar, eggs and vanilla together until thick. Stir in the chopped nuts, ground almonds, courgette and spices.
3. Sift over the bicarbonate of soda and flours and stir to combine. Pour the batter into the tin and bake for 1 hour 10 minutes or until a skewer pushed into the centre comes out clean. Cool in the tin for 20 minutes, then turn the cake out on to a wire rack and cool completely.
4. For the icing, beat the butter and sugar with an electric hand mixer until light and fluffy. With the motor running, gradually add the cream cheese, beating well between additions, then add the lime zest and juice and beat until smooth.
5. Slice the cake in half horizontally with a bread knife. Spread a third of the icing over the bottom half, then replace the top half. Spread the remaining icing over the cake, then decorate with the pistachios.

## spiced fruit cake
**Serves 12-14**

250g raisins
175g sultanas
100g candied peel, finely chopped
50g glacé cherries, halved
150ml whisky
Finely grated zest of 2 oranges
200g softened butter, plus extra to grease
180g soft dark brown sugar
4 medium free-range eggs
275g self-raising flour
½ tsp baking powder
1 tsp ground cinnamon
1 tsp mixed spice
½ tsp ground cloves
1 tsp ground ginger
100g blanched almonds, plus extra to decorate
80g apricot jam

1. Preheat the oven to 160°C/fan140°C/gas 3. Put the dried fruit, peel, cherries, whisky and zest in a pan over a low heat. Warm for 2-3 minutes, then set aside.
2. Grease a 23cm round cake tin and line the base with baking paper. Beat the butter in a stand mixer until pale. Add the sugar and beat until pale and fluffy, then add the eggs one by one, beating well after each addition.
3. Sift the flour, baking powder and spices together, then fold them into the butter and sugar. Stir in the fruit and nuts. Spoon the mixture into the tin, smooth the top and decorate with almonds.
4. Bake for 1-1½ hours until a skewer inserted into the centre comes out clean. Cool in the tin before turning out.
5. Melt the jam in a saucepan over a low heat with 1 tbsp boiling water, sieve, then brush over the cake for a glossy finish.

Courgette and pistachio spice cake with lime icing

Mascarpone
and blueberry
cheesecake

Hazelnut, cinnamon and coconut cake

## mascarpone and blueberry cheesecake

**Serves 12**

Start this recipe a day ahead, if possible: the cheesecake benefits greatly from a night in the fridge.

50g butter, melted, plus extra to grease
200g stem ginger biscuits, crushed
350g cream cheese, softened
1 vanilla pod, seeds only
400g mascarpone, softened
150g caster sugar
2 tbsp cornflour
Finely grated zest of 1 small orange
3 medium free-range eggs
250g blueberries

1. Preheat the oven to 160°C/fan140°C/gas 3. Grease a 24cm round springform cake tin.
2. Mix the biscuit crumbs with the melted butter in a bowl and press them firmly into the base of the tin, using the back of a metal spoon to level the top. Chill for 10 minutes.
3. Put the cream cheese in a stand mixer and beat until smooth. Beat in the vanilla seeds, mascarpone, sugar, cornflour and orange zest. Add the eggs, one at a time, beating well to incorporate after each addition.
4. Stir in all but a handful of the blueberries and pour the mixture into the prepared tin. Put the tin on a baking tray, then scatter the remaining blueberries over the batter and push them in lightly. Bake for 45-60 minutes until golden brown and almost set but still a little wobbly in the centre.
5. Turn the oven off, open the door slightly and leave the cheesecake to cool completely in the oven.
6. Cover and chill in the refrigerator for a few hours or overnight, then serve.

## hazelnut, cinnamon and coconut cake

**Serves 12**

185ml sunflower oil, plus extra to grease
4 medium free-range eggs
440g caster sugar
130g rice flour
150g plain flour
1 tsp baking powder
420g thick Greek-style yogurt
120g desiccated coconut
100g roasted hazelnuts, finely chopped, plus extra to serve
Cinnamon sugar to dust

1. Preheat the oven to 180°C/fan160°C/gas 4. Liberally grease a 22cm bundt tin (available at wayfair.co.uk).
2. Whisk the eggs and sugar together in a stand mixer until thick and pale. Sift the flours and baking powder into a bowl, then stir in the oil, yogurt, coconut and chopped hazelnuts until combined. Stir in the egg mixture.
3. Pour into the tin and bake for 1 hour 20 minutes or until a skewer pushed into the centre comes out clean. Leave to cool in the tin, then run a knife around the inside of the tin to loosen and remove the cake. Dust with cinnamon sugar and sprinkle with nuts before serving.

Summer fruit and hazelnut pavlova

## summer fruit and hazelnut pavlova
**Serves 12-14**

6 medium free-range egg whites
300g caster sugar
1 tsp vanilla extract
50g blanched toasted hazelnuts,
very finely chopped
2-3 tbsp clear honey
4 nectarines or peaches,
sliced into wedges
7-8 fresh lemon thyme sprigs,
plus extra to serve
150ml dessert wine, such as Sauternes
350ml double cream
2-3 tbsp icing sugar
125g raspberries

1. Preheat the oven to 120°C/fan100°C/
gas ½. Line a baking tray with baking
paper. Draw a 26cm circle in the centre.
2. Whisk the egg whites in the bowl of
a stand mixer to stiff peaks, then add
the sugar, 1 tbsp at a time, whisking
constantly until the sugar has completely
dissolved. Whisk for a further 5 minutes
or until the mixture is stiff and glossy.
Fold in the vanilla extract and hazelnuts.
3. Spoon the meringue on to the baking
paper, piling it inside the circle. Make an
indentation in the centre with the back
of the spoon. Bake in the oven for 2½
hours. Turn the oven off and leave the
meringue inside until completely cool.
4. Put a non-stick frying pan over a
medium heat, then add the honey, fruit
and thyme. Cook for 30 seconds, then
gently turn the fruit over and pour in the
wine. Bubble until the fruit is cooked but
not falling apart and the juices are
syrupy. Transfer to a bowl and cool.
5. Whip the cream until soft peaks form,
then whisk in the icing sugar. Pile the
cream over the meringue, spoon over
the nectarines and scatter with berries
and extra thyme sprigs. Drizzle with the
syrup from the fruit and serve.

## white chocolate truffle cake
**Serves 10-12**

200g butter, softened, plus extra
to grease
250g caster sugar
½ tsp vanilla extract
2 medium free-range eggs
250g self-raising flour, sifted
200ml milk
135g white chocolate, melted
7 white chocolate truffles

**FOR THE GANACHE**
375ml double cream
625g white chocolate, chopped

1. To make the ganache, warm the cream
over a low-medium heat, stirring, to just
below the boiling point. Put the chocolate
in a heatproof bowl and pour over the
cream, stirring until smooth. Cover and
chill for 6-8 hours until thickened.
2. Preheat the oven to 160°C/fan140°C/
gas 3. Grease 3 x 20cm round springform
cake tins and base line with baking paper.
3. Beat the butter and sugar with an
electric hand mixer until pale and fluffy.
Add the vanilla, then the eggs, one at a
time, beating well after each addition.
4. Mix in one-third of the flour, then half
the milk. Repeat, then beat in the rest
of the flour. Gently beat in the melted
white chocolate until combined. Divide
the mixture evenly among the 3 tins.
5. Bake for 25-30 minutes until firm and
a skewer pushed into the centre comes
out clean. (Rotate the tins halfway
through cooking, if necessary, to ensure
even baking.) Cool in the tin for 5-10
minutes, then transfer to wire racks,
remove the baking paper and cool.
6. Spread 2 of the cakes with ganache,
reserving three-quarters of the ganache
for decorating the outside of the cake,
then sandwich all the cakes together
in 3 layers. Use the remaining ganache
to cover the top and sides of the cake,
then decorate with the truffles. The iced
cake will keep in an airtight container
for up to 2 days.

White chocolate truffle cake

Dark and white chocolate
melt-in-the-middle puds, p47

# puddings

Yogurt and mixed
berry pudding, p47

Apple cinnamon crumble

## dark and white chocolate melt-in-the-middle puds
**Makes 8**

250g unsalted butter, plus extra
to grease
Icing sugar to dust
400g good-quality dark chocolate,
broken into pieces
60ml dark rum
4 medium free-range eggs, plus 4 extra
egg yolks
110g caster sugar
50g plain flour
8 white chocolate truffles

1. Preheat the oven to 180°C/fan160°C/
gas 4. Grease 8 x 175ml pudding basins
and dust with icing sugar. Shake off any
excess and put them on a baking tray.
2. Put the butter, dark chocolate and
rum in a heatproof bowl and set over
a pan of gently simmering water (don't
let the bowl touch the water). Melt
together, stirring occasionally, until
smooth. Remove the bowl from the heat
and set aside to cool completely.
3. Whisk the eggs and extra yolks with
the caster sugar in a stand mixer for
5 minutes until thick and fluffy. Carefully
fold in the cooled chocolate mix. Sift over
the flour, then fold in with a metal spoon.
4. Divide half the mixture evenly among
the 8 basins, then put a white chocolate
truffle in the centre of each. Pour over
the remaining mixture, then bake for
12 minutes or until the edges are firm
but the centres have a slight wobble.
5. Allow to stand for 2-3 minutes, then
carefully turn out each pudding on to
a plate, running a knife blade around
the edge of the basins to loosen if
necessary. Serve immediately.

## apple cinnamon crumble
**Serves 6-8**

1kg green apples, peeled and chopped
50g sultanas
50g light muscovado or demerara sugar
55g caster sugar
1 tsp ground cinnamon
Pinch of freshly grated nutmeg
½ tsp ground cloves
Butter to grease
Warm custard (see Basics,
p124) to serve

**FOR THE CRUMBLE TOPPING**
170g self-raising flour
1 tsp ground cinnamon
55g caster sugar
50g light muscovado or demerara sugar
125g cold butter, chopped

1. Preheat the oven to 200°C/fan180°C/
gas 6. To make the topping, put the flour
in a large bowl with the cinnamon and
sugars and stir, then add the butter. Rub
the butter in with your fingertips until it
resembles coarse crumbs.
2. Mix the apples, sultanas, sugars and
spices in a greased 1.4 litre ovenproof
dish, then top with the crumble mixture.
3. Bake for 30 minutes, then cool for
10 minutes before serving with plenty
of warm custard.

## yogurt and mixed berry pudding
**Serves 6-8**

50g butter, softened, plus
extra to grease
125g caster sugar
300g fresh or thawed mixed berries
2 medium free-range eggs
100g thick Greek-style yogurt,
plus extra to serve
125g self-raising flour, sifted
2 tbsp flaked almonds
Icing sugar to dust

1. Preheat the oven to 160°C/fan140°C/
gas 3. Grease the base of an 800ml
baking dish. Mix 2 tbsp of the caster
sugar with the berries and spoon into
the baking dish.
2. Use a stand mixer to beat together
the butter and remaining sugar until
pale and creamy. Add the eggs, one at
a time, beating well after each addition.
Fold the yogurt and flour into the egg
mixture in 3 batches, alternating
between the two, until smooth.
3. Spoon the mixture over the berries,
smooth the top, then scatter with the
almonds. Bake for 40-45 minutes until
the sponge is golden and springs back
when lightly touched. Dust with icing
sugar and serve warm with extra yogurt.

Chocolate and panettone pudding

## sticky mandarin steamed puddings
**Makes 6**

Butter to grease
Brown sugar to sprinkle
1 mandarin, thinly sliced into rounds, plus the juice of 1 mandarin
125g self-raising flour
90g caster sugar
70g fresh breadcrumbs
1 tsp baking powder
90g vegetable suet
115g marmalade
2½ tsp ground ginger
1 tsp ground cinnamon
1 medium free-range egg
115g golden syrup
60-80ml milk

**FOR THE SYRUP**
Juice of 2 mandarins, strained
75g caster sugar
2 tbsp golden syrup

1. Grease 6 x 175ml dariole moulds or pudding basins and sprinkle with brown sugar. Put a mandarin round in the bottom of each.
2. Mix the flour, sugar, breadcrumbs, baking powder, suet and a pinch of salt in a bowl. Whisk together the mandarin juice, marmalade, spices, egg and syrup in a second bowl. Stir this into the flour with just enough milk to give a soft dropping consistency.
3. Divide the batter between the moulds, filling each two-thirds full. Cover with a circle of baking paper, tying string under the rim to secure it and using a longer piece of string to make a handle. Put the moulds in a large pan, pour in boiling water to halfway up their sides, then bring to the boil. Cover and reduce the heat to low. Steam for 30-40 minutes, topping up the water if required.
4. Meanwhile, put the syrup ingredients in a pan over a medium heat, stirring until the sugar melts. Increase the heat and boil until thick and syrupy. Cool the puddings in the moulds for 5 minutes, then turn out and drizzle with the syrup. Allow the syrup to soak in before serving.

## chocolate and panettone pudding
**Serves 8-10**

Butter to grease
750g fruit panettone, sliced into thin wedges
100ml amaretto liqueur
100g good-quality dark chocolate, roughly chopped
4 medium free-range eggs
30g caster sugar
900ml double cream, plus extra to serve

1. Grease a large ovenproof dish and arrange half the panettone in the base, with the slices overlapping. Drizzle with half the amaretto, then scatter over half the chopped dark chocolate. Repeat with the remaining panettone, amaretto and chocolate.
2. Mix the eggs and sugar in a large bowl, then whisk in the cream. Pour the cream mixture evenly over the top of the panettone, then allow it to stand at room temperature for at least 30 minutes. Meanwhile, preheat the oven to 180°C/fan160°C/gas 4.
3. Bake for 25 minutes or until puffed and golden. Remove from the oven and allow to rest for 10 minutes before serving warm with extra double cream.

Sticky mandarin
steamed puddings

Pear and cranberry
clafoutis

## pear and cranberry clafoutis

**Serves 4**

This is a winter version of the classic French batter pudding.

3 medium free-range eggs,
plus 2 egg yolks
75g caster sugar
30g plain flour, sifted
250ml milk
½ tsp vanilla extract
100g dried cranberries
60ml port, Marsala or poire william liqueur
Butter to grease
2 ripe pears
2 tbsp flaked almonds
Icing sugar to dust

1. Use an electric hand mixer to beat the eggs, egg yolks and sugar together in a large bowl for 2 minutes or until pale and creamy. Gently fold in the flour and a pinch of salt, then add the milk and vanilla, mixing lightly until you have a smooth batter. Chill for 30 minutes.
2. Meanwhile, put the cranberries in a small bowl. Cover with the wine or liqueur, then leave to soak for 30 minutes. Drain, reserving the liquid.
3. Preheat the oven to 190°C/fan170°C/gas 5. Grease a shallow 26cm x 18cm baking dish. Peel the pears, quarter them lengthways, then remove the core. Arrange in the baking dish and scatter with most of the drained cranberries.
4. Stir the batter and pour it over the fruit (it won't cover it completely). Scatter with the flaked almonds and bake for 20-25 minutes until the top is golden and the inside is wobbly like a just-set custard.
5. Remove the clafoutis from the oven and leave it to set for 5 minutes, then scatter the top with the remaining cranberries. Just before serving, dust the top with icing sugar and drizzle with the reserved wine or liqueur from the cranberries, if you like.

Baked pear crumble with chocolate sauce

## baked pear crumble with chocolate sauce

**Serves 4**

4 ripe pears, halved, cores removed with a teaspoon
90g rolled oats
75g plain flour
½ tsp ground cinnamon
55g caster sugar
60g light brown muscovado sugar
80g butter, softened

FOR THE CHOCOLATE SAUCE
150g good-quality dark chocolate, broken into pieces
45g butter, softened

1. Preheat the oven to 200°C/fan180°C/gas 6. Put the pears cut-side up on a baking tray lined with baking paper.
2. Put the oats, flour, cinnamon and sugars in a large bowl. Using your fingertips, rub in the butter until the mixture resembles coarse crumbs.
3. Press the crumble on to the cut side of the pears. Bake for 40 minutes or until the pears are tender and the crumble topping is golden brown.
4. Meanwhile, put the chocolate for the sauce in a heatproof bowl set over, but not touching, a pan of simmering water. Stir occasionally until melted, stir in the butter until it forms a smooth sauce, then drizzle on top of the pears to serve.

Tropical fruit crumble

## tropical fruit crumble
**Serves 6**

120g soft light muscovado sugar
200g plain flour
150g chilled butter, chopped
50g shredded coconut
75g macadamia nuts, toasted and
roughly chopped
Finely grated zest of 1 lime

FOR THE FILLING
1 large supersweet pineapple,
peeled, core removed, cut into
bite-size pieces
Finely grated zest and juice
of 1 orange
110g caster sugar
1 tbsp arrowroot
Pulp and seeds of 3 passion fruit

1. Preheat the oven to 180°C/fan160°C/
gas 4. To make the filling, put the
pineapple in a pan with the orange zest
and juice and the caster sugar. Bring to
a simmer over a medium heat and cook,
stirring occasionally, for 5-8 minutes
until the pineapple starts to soften.
2. Mix the arrowroot with 2 tsp water.
Add to the pan and bring to a simmer,
then remove the pan from the heat and
pour it into a 2 litre baking dish. Top with
the passion fruit pulp and seeds.
3. To make the crumble, put the sugar
and flour in a bowl. Rub in the butter
until the mixture resembles fine
breadcrumbs. Fold in the coconut,
chopped nuts and lime zest. Spread the
crumble over the fruit and bake for 30
minutes or until the crumble is golden
and the fruit underneath is bubbling.

## jam and chocolate
## roly poly with custard
**Serves 6-8**

150g self-raising flour, plus extra
to dust
2 tbsp caster sugar
75g shredded suet
½ tsp salt
100ml milk, plus extra for brushing
200g good-quality raspberry jam
50g chopped dark chocolate
Butter to grease
Custard (see Basics, p124), warmed
to serve

1. Sift the flour into a bowl, then stir
in the sugar, suet and salt. Add the milk
and stir to form a soft dough.
2. Roll out the dough on a lightly floured
surface into a 30cm x 20cm rectangle.
Spread with the jam, leaving a 2cm
border on all sides. Sprinkle with the
chocolate, brush a little milk on the
pastry border, then roll it up tightly,
starting with one of the long sides,
to form a long roll.
3. Lightly grease a sheet of baking paper,
fold a pleat down the centre, then put the
roly poly, seam-side down, on the baking
paper. Roll it up in the paper, tucking in
the ends. Take a sheet of foil, fold a pleat
down the centre, then use to wrap the
roly poly, twisting the ends to seal.
4. Put the roly poly in a large steamer
or on a rack in a fish kettle with a little
water in the bottom. Steam for 1 hour,
topping up the water if required, until
the roly poly springs back when lightly
touched (pull back the foil and paper to
check). Remove from the steamer/fish
kettle and leave to stand for 10 minutes.
Remove the foil and baking paper, then
serve with warm custard (see Basics,
p124, for how to make).

Jam and chocolate
roly poly with custard

Spiced chocolate
bread puddings

Upside-down cranberry
and pecan puddings

## spiced chocolate bread puddings
**Makes 8**

600ml double cream
250ml whole milk
2 cinnamon sticks
1 tsp vanilla extract
150g milk chocolate, chopped
100g dark chilli chocolate, chopped
75g caster sugar
4 medium free-range egg yolks
2 tbsp dark rum
400g brioche loaf, cut into 1cm dice
Butter to grease
150ml crème fraîche
1 tbsp icing sugar, plus extra to serve
Shaved chocolate and ground
cinnamon to serve

1. Put 500ml of the cream in a pan over a medium heat with the milk, cinnamon and vanilla, then bring to a simmer.
2. Put both chopped chocolates in a bowl, then pour over the hot cream mixture and stir well. Put the caster sugar and yolks in a separate bowl and whisk until pale. Add the chocolate cream to the egg yolks, then whisk to combine. Stir in the rum.
3. Put the brioche in a large bowl. Strain the chocolate mixture on top and leave it to absorb the liquid for 30 minutes, pressing it down occasionally.
4. Preheat the oven to 180°C/fan160°C/gas 4 and lightly grease 8 x 200ml ovenproof cups or ramekins. Divide the brioche mixture between the cups and put them in a deep roasting tin. Pour in enough boiling water to come halfway up the sides of the cups and bake for 25 minutes until the custard has just set.
5. Meanwhile, beat the remaining cream with the crème fraîche and icing sugar until soft peaks form. Spoon on to the cooked puddings and top with chocolate shavings, cinnamon and icing sugar.

## upside-down cranberry and pecan puddings
**Serves 4**

100g butter, softened
110g caster sugar
Finely grated zest of 1 small orange
2 medium free-range eggs,
lightly beaten
50g self-raising flour
1 tsp baking powder
60g ground almonds
Custard (see Basics, p124),
warmed, to serve (optional)

**FOR THE TOPPING**
30g butter, softened
30g brown sugar
24 pecan halves
100g fresh or thawed cranberries

1. Preheat the oven to 180°C/fan160°C/gas 4. To make the topping, mix the butter and sugar and spread it over the bases of 4 x 250ml metal pudding basins. Arrange the pecans and cranberries on top. Set aside.
2. Put the butter and sugar in a stand mixer and beat until pale and fluffy. Beat in the orange zest.
3. Gradually beat in the eggs, adding a small spoonful of flour with the last addition. Sift over the remaining flour and baking powder, then gently fold into the mixture with the ground almonds.
4. Divide the mixture between the basins and bake for 25 minutes or until a skewer poked into the centre comes out clean.
5. Run a knife around each pudding and turn out on to serving plates. Serve with warm custard, if desired.

Double chocolate cupcakes, p59

# cupcakes

Banana cupcakes with
soured cream icing, p59

Cheesecake cupcakes

## cheesecake cupcakes
**Makes 12**

120g digestive biscuits, finely crushed
75g unsalted butter, melted
350g ricotta, at room
temperature
350g cream cheese, at room
temperature
2 tsp vanilla extract
150g icing sugar, sifted
2 medium free-range eggs
50g good-quality dark chocolate,
melted
125g blueberries

1. Preheat the oven to 160°C/fan140°C/
gas 3. Line a 12-hole muffin tin with
paper muffin cases.
2. Mix the crushed biscuits and butter
together in a bowl. Divide the biscuit
crumb between the cases, pressing it
down firmly into the bases. Chill for
10 minutes to set.
3. Beat the ricotta, cream cheese,
vanilla and sugar in a stand mixer until
smooth. Add the eggs, one at a time,
beating constantly on low speed. Spoon
the batter into the cases, filling them
to the top. Bake for 30-35 minutes until
the surface is set, but the cupcake
centres have a slight wobble.
4. Leave the cupcakes to cool in the tin
for 5 minutes, then transfer to a wire
rack to cool completely. Drizzle the
cakes with the melted chocolate and
top with the blueberries to serve.

## banana cupcakes with soured cream icing
**Makes 12**

70g unsalted butter
150g caster sugar
150g plain flour, sifted
1½ tsp baking powder
125g puréed banana (about 2)
125ml buttermilk
½ tsp vanilla extract
1 medium free-range egg
Freshly grated nutmeg to serve

**FOR THE ICING**
300ml soured cream, at room
temperature
2 tbsp caster sugar
½ tsp vanilla extract

1. Preheat the oven to 170°C/fan150°C/
gas 3½. Line a 12-hole muffin tin with
paper muffin cases. Put the butter and
sugar in a stand mixer and beat until
pale and fluffy. Stir in the flour, baking
powder and banana until combined.
2. In a separate bowl, whisk together
the buttermilk, vanilla and egg, then
beat this into the banana mixture.
3. Divide the batter among the cases
and bake for 20-25 minutes until golden
and a skewer pushed into the centre of
the cakes comes out clean. Allow to cool
for 5 minutes in the tin, then transfer to
a wire rack and allow to cool completely.
4. To make the icing, put the ingredients
in a bowl and stir to combine. Spoon this
on to the cooled cakes and serve topped
with freshly grated nutmeg.

## double chocolate cupcakes
**Makes 12**

250g brown sugar
50g cocoa powder
50g good-quality dark chocolate,
roughly chopped, plus flakes to serve
150ml milk
100g butter, chopped
2 medium free-range eggs
225g plain flour
1 tsp bicarbonate of soda

**FOR THE TOPPING**
60ml double cream
200g good-quality dark
chocolate, chopped

1. Preheat the oven to 180°C/fan160°C/
gas 4. Line a 12-hole muffin tin with
paper muffin cases.
2. Put the sugar, cocoa, 50g chocolate,
milk and butter into a large heatproof
bowl set over a pan of simmering water
and heat, stirring, until the chocolate
and butter have melted. Leave to cool
slightly, then beat in the eggs.
3. Sift the flour and bicarbonate of soda
into the mixture and stir until smooth.
Divide the batter between the cases and
bake for 20-25 minutes until risen and
a skewer pushed in the centre comes out
clean. Cool in the tin for 5 minutes, then
transfer to a rack to cool completely.
4. To make the topping, put the cream
and chocolate in a heatproof bowl over
a pan of simmering water and stir until
the chocolate melts. Set aside for
20 minutes, then spread over each cake
and top with the chocolate flakes.

**cupcakes.**

Vanilla cupcakes with
black cherry icing

### vanilla cupcakes with black cherry icing
**Makes 12**

185g plain flour, sifted
185g caster sugar
2 tsp baking powder
1 tsp vanilla extract
80g butter, softened
125ml buttermilk
2 medium free-range eggs

**FOR THE ICING**
120g black cherries in syrup (we like Opies)
125g icing sugar, sifted
75g butter, softened

1. Preheat the oven to 170°C/fan150°C/ gas 3½. Line a 12-hole muffin tin with paper muffin cases.
2. Put the flour, sugar, baking powder, vanilla, butter and a pinch of salt in a stand mixer and beat on a low speed for 5 minutes until it forms coarse crumbs.

3. Beat in the buttermilk, then add the eggs, one at a time, beating well after each addition. Increase the mixer speed to medium and beat until you have a smooth batter. Spoon this into the cases, filling each half full, then bake for 20-25 minutes until a skewer pushed into the centre comes out clean.
4. Leave the cakes to cool for 5 minutes in the tin, then transfer them to a wire rack to cool completely.
5. Meanwhile, to make the icing, whizz 25ml cherry syrup with 35g of the black cherries in a blender to make a smooth purée (reserve the remaining cherries to decorate). Beat the sugar and butter in a stand mixer on a medium speed until smooth, then increase the speed to medium-high and beat for 5 minutes or until pale and fluffy. Fold in the cherry purée, then spoon the icing into a piping bag fitted with a star nozzle and pipe over the cakes, or spread the icing over them with a palette knife. Top the iced cakes with the remaining cherries.

### party cupcakes
**Makes 12**

220g caster sugar
2 medium free-range eggs
90g butter, melted
300g self-raising flour
250ml milk
Jelly beans to decorate

**FOR THE WHITE CHOCOLATE ICING**
300g white chocolate, chopped
90g butter, chopped
90ml double cream

1. Preheat the oven to 170°C/fan150°C/ gas 3½. Line a 12-hole muffin tin with paper muffin cases.
2. Beat the sugar, eggs and butter together with an electric hand mixer until pale and creamy. Sift in half the flour, then fold in half the milk, then repeat with the remaining flour and milk, folding until well combined. Divide the mixture between the cases, then bake for 20 minutes. Leave to cool.
3. Meanwhile make the icing. Put the white chocolate and butter in a heatproof bowl. Put the cream in a pan over a medium heat and bring to just below boiling. Pour the cream over the chocolate and leave, without stirring, for 1 minute, then stir until smooth. Put over a pan of boiling water if it hasn't fully melted (don't let the bowl touch the water). Leave to cool completely, chill for 1 hour, then beat well until smooth.
4. Spoon the icing into a piping bag fitted with a star nozzle and pipe it over the cupcakes, or spread it over each cake with a palette knife. Decorate with jelly beans and serve.

Party cupcakes

Coconut and lime
meringue cupcakes

## coconut and lime meringue cupcakes
**Makes 10-12**

160g plain flour, sifted
3 tsp baking powder, sifted
155g caster sugar
65g butter, softened
2 medium free-range eggs
125ml coconut milk
Finely grated zest of 1 lime,
plus juice of ½ lime
65g desiccated coconut

FOR THE MERINGUE
2 medium free-range egg whites
125g caster sugar
Finely grated zest of ½ lime and a
squeeze of juice

1. Preheat the oven to 170°C/fan150°C/
gas 3½ and line 12 holes of a muffin tin
with paper muffin cases.
2. Put the flour, baking powder, sugar,
butter and a pinch of salt in a stand
mixer and beat on a low speed for
5 minutes until you have coarse crumbs.
Add the eggs, one at a time, beating well
after each addition. Add the coconut
milk, lime zest and juice, then beat until
smooth. Fold the coconut into the
mixture, then divide between the cases.
3. Bake for 20-25 minutes until the
cakes are golden and a skewer pushed
into the centre comes out clean. Cool
in the tin for 5 minutes, then transfer
to a wire rack to cool completely.
4. For the meringue, whisk the egg
whites until soft peaks form, then add
the sugar, 1 tbsp at a time, whisking
constantly until stiff and glossy. Add
a squeeze of lime juice, fold in the zest,
then put the meringue in a piping bag
fitted with a plain nozzle. Pipe on to the
cakes, then use a kitchen blowtorch
to cook the meringue until golden.
Alternatively, bake the meringue-topped
cakes at 200°C/fan180°C/gas 6 for
another 5-10 minutes until browned.

Tiramisu cupcakes

## tiramisu cupcakes
**Makes 12**

125g butter, softened
150g caster sugar
2 medium free-range eggs
2 tsp espresso coffee, cooled
1 tsp vanilla extract
200g plain flour, sifted
2 tsp baking powder
125ml milk
Cocoa powder and nougat pieces
to serve

FOR THE ICING
400g icing sugar, sifted
150g butter, softened
2-3 tsp espresso coffee, cooled

1. Preheat the oven to 180°C/fan160°C/
gas 4. Line a 12-hole muffin tin with
paper muffin cases. Beat the butter and
sugar in a stand mixer until pale and
fluffy. Add the eggs, one at a time, beating
well after each, then add the 2 tsp
espresso and the vanilla and mix well.
2. Sift together the flour and baking
powder. In 3 batches, alternately add the
flour and milk to the mix, beating after
each addition until smooth. Spoon into
the cases and bake for 15-20 minutes
until golden and a skewer pushed into
the centre comes out clean. Cool for
5 minutes in the tin, then transfer to
a rack to cool completely.
3. Meanwhile, for the icing, beat the
sugar and butter in a stand mixer until
pale and fluffy. Add the espresso to
taste, then mix well. Spoon the icing into
a piping bag fitted with a star nozzle and
pipe on to the cupcakes. Top with nougat
pieces and dust with cocoa, then serve.

Strawberry
cupcakes

## orange and almond cupcakes with greek yogurt
**Makes 12**

150g butter, softened
150g caster sugar
3 medium free-range eggs, separated
250g ground almonds
Finely grated zest of 1 orange, plus
100ml juice
Icing sugar and Greek yogurt to serve

1. Preheat the oven to 180°C/fan160°C/
gas 4 and line a 12-hole muffin tin with
paper muffin cases.
2. Beat the butter and 100g sugar in
a stand mixer until thick and pale. Add
the egg yolks, one at a time, beating
well after each addition. Fold in the
ground almonds. Add the orange zest
and juice, then mix to combine.
3. Meanwhile, whisk the egg whites
in a clean bowl until soft peaks form.
Whisk in the remaining 50g caster
sugar, 1 tbsp at a time, until the
mixture is stiff and glossy.
4. Fold the whisked egg whites into the
batter in 3 batches. Divide the batter
between the paper cases. Bake for
20 minutes until golden and a skewer
pushed into the centre comes out clean.
Allow the cakes to cool in the tin for
5 minutes, then transfer to a wire rack
to cool completely.
5. Dust with icing sugar and serve with
a spoonful of Greek yogurt on top.

## strawberry cupcakes
**Makes 12**
These gorgeous cupcakes can be
stored, without the cream topping,
in an airtight container for 1-2 days.

225g plain flour, sifted
2 tsp baking powder
110g butter, softened
220g caster sugar
2 medium free-range eggs
1 tsp vanilla extract
125ml milk
250g strawberries, finely chopped
185ml double cream
3 tbsp strawberry jam

1. Preheat the oven to 170°C/fan150°C/
gas 3½ and line a 12-hole muffin tin

with paper muffin cases. Sift the flour,
baking powder and a pinch of salt into
a bowl and set aside.
2. Beat the butter and sugar in a stand
mixer until pale and fluffy. Add the eggs,
one at a time, beating well after each
addition. Stir through the vanilla.
3. Fold in the flour and milk in
3 batches, alternating between
the two. Fold in 200g of the chopped
strawberries, then divide the batter
between the cases. Bake for 25-30
minutes until golden and a skewer
pushed into the centre comes out clean.
4. Whip the cream to soft peaks and fold
in half the jam. Combine the remaining
jam with the remaining strawberries.
Spoon the cream on top of the cakes and
serve topped with the remaining fruit.

Orange and almond
cupcakes with Greek yogurt

Courgette and almond muffins, p69

# muffins and scones

Lemonade scones, p69

Corn and bacon muffins

## courgette and almond muffins
**Makes 16**

250g coarsely grated courgette
(about 2 courgettes)
110g sultanas
80ml orange juice
2 tbsp honey
3 medium free-range eggs
175ml sunflower oil
200g brown sugar
225g self-raising flour, sifted
½ tsp baking powder
½ tsp bicarbonate of soda
55g blanched almonds, toasted and
roughly chopped
Finely grated zest of 2 limes

**FOR THE ICING**
250g cream cheese, softened
50g icing sugar, sifted
Juice of 2 limes, plus finely
grated zest to sprinkle
Finely chopped blanched almonds
to sprinkle

1. Preheat the oven to 180°C/fan160°C/
gas 4. Line 16 muffin-tin holes with
paper cases. Squeeze the grated
courgette to drain any excess moisture
and pat dry with a paper towel.
2. Put the sultanas in a small saucepan
with the orange juice and honey. Bring
to the boil over a medium-high heat,
reduce the heat to medium-low, then
simmer for 4 minutes (be careful not to
let it burn) until the sultanas are plump
and the liquid is absorbed. Set aside.
3. Beat the eggs, oil and sugar in
a stand mixer for 3 minutes until
creamy. Add the flour, baking powder,
bicarbonate of soda, almonds, zest,
courgette and sultanas. Mix until just
combined. Spoon into the cases, then
bake for 25-30 minutes until a skewer
pushed into the centre comes out clean.
Cool in the tin for 5 minutes, then
transfer to a rack to cool completely.
4. Beat the cream cheese, icing sugar
and lime juice until smooth, adding more
icing sugar to taste. Spread over the
muffins, then sprinkle with zest and nuts.

## corn and bacon muffins
**Makes 22**

50ml sunflower oil, plus extra
to grease
1 small onion, finely chopped
300g bacon, chopped
310g tin sweetcorn, drained
300ml natural yogurt
1 medium free-range egg, beaten
1 courgette, grated
125g polenta
150g plain flour
3 tsp baking powder
Black olives and cheese (optional)
to serve

1. Preheat the oven to 190°C/fan170°C/
gas 5 and grease 22 muffin-tin holes.
2. Heat the oil in a frying pan over a
medium heat. Add the onion and cook,
stirring, for 2-3 minutes until softened.
Add the bacon and cook for 5 minutes
or until starting to crisp, then add the
corn and cook for 1 minute more.
Transfer to a bowl and set aside to cool.
3. Once cooled, add the yogurt, egg,
courgette and polenta to the bowl. Sift in
the flour and baking powder. Mix until
just combined (don't overmix).
4. Divide among the prepared muffin
holes and bake for 25 minutes or until
golden. Cool slightly in the tin, then turn
out onto a rack. Serve warm with olives
and cheese, if you like.

## lemonade scones
**Makes 28**

300g self-raising flour, sifted, plus
extra to dust
1 tsp baking powder
2 tbsp caster sugar, plus extra
Finely grated zest of 1 lemon
½ tsp salt
125ml double cream, plus extra
to brush and to serve
125ml lemonade
Jam to serve

1. Preheat the oven to 220°C/fan200°C/
gas 7 and line a large baking sheet with
baking paper. Put the flour, baking
powder, sugar, lemon zest and salt in
a large bowl. Add the cream and
lemonade and mix to form a soft dough.
2. Turn out onto a lightly floured surface
and knead 5-10 times. Pat flat to 2cm
thick. Use a 5cm round cutter dusted in
flour to cut 28 scones from the dough.
3. Put the scones on the baking sheet,
then brush the tops lightly with double
cream. Sprinkle with sugar, then bake
for 10-12 minutes until lightly browned.
Allow to cool on a wire rack, then serve
with double cream and jam.

Orange and date muffins

### orange and date muffins
**Makes 12**

150g unsalted butter, melted, plus extra
to grease
350g plain flour, sifted
2 tsp baking powder
1 tsp bicarbonate of soda
½ tsp salt
45g whole pecans
140g whole dates, roughly chopped
60g light muscovado sugar
1 orange, unpeeled, roughly chopped,
seeds removed
125ml (2-3 oranges) fresh orange juice
2 medium free-range eggs

1. Preheat the oven to 180°C/fan160°C/
gas 4 and grease a 12-hole muffin tin.

Sift the flour, baking powder, bicarbonate
of soda and salt into a mixing bowl. Set
aside 12 pecans and roughly chop the
rest. Add the chopped pecans and dates
to the bowl and toss to coat in the flour.
2. Add the sugar and mix. Put the
chopped orange and juice in a food
processor and blitz until the peel is
finely chopped. Add the eggs and pulse
to combine. Add the contents of the
food processor to the flour with the
melted butter, then stir to combine.
3. Spoon into the prepared tin, top each
muffin with a whole pecan and bake
for 25-30 minutes until golden and
a skewer pushed into the centre comes
out clean. Cool in the tin for 5 minutes,
then transfer the muffins to a wire rack
to cool completely. Serve with butter.

### feta and olive scones
**Makes 18**

85g chilled unsalted butter, chopped,
plus extra to grease
400g self-raising flour, plus extra to dust
40g pitted black olives, chopped
40g sun-dried tomatoes, drained and
chopped
85g feta, crumbled
2 tsp finely chopped fresh rosemary
200ml milk, plus extra to brush

1. Preheat the oven to 220°C/fan200°C/
gas 7 and grease a baking tray. Sift the
flour into a bowl and grind over lots of
black pepper. Rub in the butter with
your fingers until the mixture resembles
fine breadcrumbs.
2. Stir in the other ingredients, adding
enough milk to form a smooth dough.
Roll out on a lightly floured surface to a
rectangle 3cm thick. Cut into 10 squares.
Put on the baking tray, brush with a little
more milk, then bake for 12 minutes until
golden and cooked through. Serve warm.

Feta and olive scones

Cranberry and
pistachio scones

Lemon friands

## cranberry and pistachio scones

**Makes 8**

300g plain flour, sifted,
plus extra to dust
75g caster sugar
1 tbsp baking powder
½ tsp salt
120g chilled unsalted butter, chopped,
plus extra to serve
165ml milk, plus extra to brush
75g dried cranberries
75g pistachios, roughly chopped

1. Preheat the oven to 220°C/fan200°C/
gas 7. Line a large baking tray with
baking paper.
2. Mix the flour, caster sugar, baking
powder and salt together in a large
bowl. Rub in the butter using your
fingertips until the mixture resembles
coarse breadcrumbs.
3. Add the milk, cranberries and
pistachios and mix to combine. Turn the
dough out onto a well-floured surface
and knead gently 5-10 times. Pat the
dough flat and shape into a 3cm-thick
circle. Cut the dough into 8 wedges
using a lightly floured knife and place
the wedges on the prepared baking tray,
spaced 3cm apart.
4. Lightly brush the tops with milk, then
bake for 12-15 minutes until golden.
Allow to cool slightly. Serve with butter.

## lemon friands

**Makes 12**
These will keep for 2-3 days in an
airtight container in a cool dark place.

190g unsalted butter
60g plain flour, plus extra to dust
200g icing sugar,
plus extra to dust
125g ground almonds
5 medium free-range egg whites
Finely grated zest of 1 lemon

1. Preheat the oven to 180°C/fan160°C/
gas 4. Melt the butter and use a little to
grease a 12-hole friand or muffin tin.
Dust with flour and shake out any excess.
2. Sift the flour and sugar into a large
bowl, then stir in the ground almonds.
Put the egg whites in a small bowl and
lightly froth with a fork. Add the egg
whites to the dry ingredients together
with the remaining melted butter and
lemon zest, stirring until the mixture is
completely combined.
3. Fill each muffin/friand hole two-thirds
full with batter. Bake for 25-35 minutes
until golden and a skewer pushed into
the centre comes out clean. Cool in the
tin for 5 minutes, then turn out onto
a wire rack to cool completely. Dust
with icing sugar before serving.

Strawberry surprise muffins

## strawberry surprise muffins

**Makes 12**

These sugar-topped treats may look like ordinary muffins but their centres hold a succulent surprise.

375g self-raising flour
1½ tsp bicarbonate of soda
150g golden caster sugar, plus extra to sprinkle
250g white chocolate, roughly chopped
3 medium free-range eggs, lightly beaten
150g unsalted butter, melted
200g natural yogurt
2 tbsp milk
12 strawberries, hulled

1. Preheat the oven to 200°C/fan180°C/gas 6 and line a 12-hole muffin tin with paper cases.
2. Mix the flour, bicarbonate of soda, caster sugar and chocolate in a large bowl with a pinch of salt.
3. In another bowl, beat the eggs, melted butter, yogurt and milk, then stir briskly into the dry ingredients. Do not overmix or the muffins will be tough (don't worry if the mixture is a bit lumpy).
4. Divide the mixture among the paper cases, then push a strawberry into each muffin, making sure it's submerged.
5. Sprinkle with the extra sugar, then bake for 20-25 minutes until golden and a skewer pushed into the centre comes out clean. Cool in the tin for 5 minutes before cooling completely on a rack.

## chocolate cherry friands

**Makes 14**

240g jar of black cherries, drained
100g unsalted butter
100g good-quality dark chocolate, chopped
6 medium free-range egg whites
100g ground hazelnuts
2 tsp vanilla extract
135g icing sugar, sifted
75g plain flour, sifted
Cocoa powder to dust
Ice cream to serve

1. Preheat the oven to 190°C/fan170°C/gas 5. Grease 14 holes of a muffin tin or friand tin. Chop half the cherries and set the remaining cherries aside to garnish. Melt the butter and chocolate in a bowl set over a pan of gently simmering water (be careful not to let the bowl touch the water). Stir until melted and smooth, then cool slightly.
2. Lightly froth the egg whites in a bowl with a fork, then add the ground hazelnuts, vanilla extract, icing sugar, flour, chopped cherries and cooled melted chocolate. Mix with a wooden spoon until combined.
3. Divide the batter among the prepared muffin/friand holes and bake for 25 minutes until risen and cooked through.
4. Cool slightly. Dust with cocoa powder and serve with ice cream and the remaining whole cherries.

Chocolate cherry friands

Cinnamon and
raisin swirls, p79

# pastries

Roasted peach and honey
puff pastry tart, p79

Classic almond
pastries

## classic almond pastries
**Serves 6**

100g butter, softened
110g caster sugar
1 medium free-range egg, beaten,
plus 2 yolks
100g almonds, toasted and ground
1 tsp almond extract
2 tbsp plain flour, plus extra to dust
1 quantity Danish pastry dough (see
Basics, p124) or 500g block ready-made
all-butter puff pastry
50g icing sugar
2 tsp milk
40g flaked almonds

1. Beat the butter and caster sugar in a
stand mixer for 5 minutes until pale and
fluffy. Beat in the 2 egg yolks, then fold
in the ground almonds, almond extract
and flour. Stir until smooth, then chill.
2. Preheat the oven to 200°C/fan180°C/
gas 6 and line a baking tray with baking
paper. Roll out the pastry on a floured
surface to a rough 45cm square, then
trim the edges to make a neat 40cm
square. Cut in half, so you have
2 rectangles of 40cm x 20cm. Spread the
almond filling down the centre of each
in a long strip, leaving a 7cm border at
the sides and a 3cm border at each end.
Fold over the uncovered 3cm pastry at
the ends to partially cover the almond
mixture, then gently press down to seal.
3. Make diagonal herringbone-style cuts
in the pastry along the sides, up to the
filling, 1cm apart, cutting all the way
through. Brush the cut pastry with
beaten egg. Fold the strips alternately
over the filling, crossing them over in
the middle. Put the pastries on the lined
tray. Cover and chill for 20 minutes.
4. Brush each pastry plait with beaten
egg and bake for 18-20 minutes until
golden brown. Meanwhile, whisk the
icing sugar and milk in a bowl to form
a thick but pourable icing. Set aside.
5. Allow the pastries to cool for 5
minutes, then drizzle with icing, scatter
with flaked almonds and slice to serve.

## roasted peach and honey puff pastry tart
**Serves 4**

375g sheet ready-rolled all-butter puff
pastry
Plain flour for dusting
1 medium free-range egg, beaten
400g tin peach slices in syrup
20g butter
Pinch of ground cinnamon
2 tbsp honey
Mascarpone to serve

1. Preheat the oven to 220°C/fan200°C/
gas 7. Put the pastry on a lightly floured
baking tray, then prick all over with a
fork and brush with beaten egg.
2. Bake for 10 minutes, uncovered, then
cover the pastry with a piece of baking
paper and another baking tray. Bake for
a further 10 minutes until golden and
cooked through. Cool slightly.
3. Drain the peaches, reserving the
syrup. Heat a frying pan over
a medium-high heat and add the butter,
cinnamon, honey, peaches and 80ml of
the reserved syrup. Simmer for
3-5 minutes until slightly reduced.
4. Remove the top baking tray and
baking paper from the pastry. Put the
pastry on a serving plate, arrange the
peaches on top and pour over the syrup.
Slice the tart into 4 generous pieces and
serve with mascarpone.

## cinnamon and raisin swirls
**Makes 16**

375g block all-butter puff pastry
Plain flour for dusting
80g butter, softened
80g caster sugar, plus extra to sprinkle
2 tsp ground cinnamon
55g raisins
1 medium free-range egg, beaten
with 2 tbsp milk

1. Preheat the oven to 200°C/fan180°C/
gas 6. Line 2 large baking trays with
baking paper.
2. Roll out the pastry on a lightly floured
surface into a rectangle measuring
about 40cm x 30cm.
3. Put the butter, sugar and cinnamon
in a bowl and use a spoon to mix until
smooth. Spread the cinnamon butter
over the pastry, scatter with the raisins,
then roll up the rectangle, starting from
a short side, to make a log. Chill for
10 minutes or until completely firm.
4. Using a serrated knife, cut the log
into 16 x 1.5cm slices. Put cut-side
down on the lined trays and flatten
slightly so they spread out a little.
Chill for 20 minutes.
5. Brush the swirls with the egg mix,
sprinkle with sugar, then bake for
18-20 minutes until golden. Serve warm.

Hot camembert
pastry parcels

## thai chicken parcels
**Makes 30 canapés**

1 tbsp olive oil
2 shallots, finely chopped
2 garlic cloves, finely chopped
2 lemongrass stalks (inner core only),
finely chopped
4 x free-range chicken breasts, minced
in a food processor
2 tbsp finely chopped fresh coriander
Pinch of chilli flakes
Flour to dust
2 x 375g blocks all-butter puff pastry
1 medium free-range egg, beaten

1. Preheat the oven to 200°C/fan180°C/
gas 6. Line 2 large baking trays with
baking paper.
2. Heat the oil in a pan over a medium
heat. Add the shallots, garlic and
lemongrass and cook, stirring, for
5 minutes or until soft. Transfer to
a bowl and leave to cool.
3. Add the chicken, coriander and chilli
flakes to the bowl and season well.
Mix well with damp hands, then shape
into 30 walnut-size balls. Flatten slightly
and chill until needed.
4. On a lightly floured surface, roll out
the pastry to form 2 large rectangles
measuring 40cm x 24cm. Cut each one
into 15 x 8cm squares.
5. Put a ball of filling in the centre of
each square. Brush the edges with
beaten egg and bring the corners
together over the filling to form a parcel.
Gently pinch the edges to seal. Brush
with egg, then chill for 15 minutes.
6. Put the parcels on the baking trays,
spaced 2-3cm apart, and bake for
25-30 minutes until golden. Cool slightly
on a wire rack, then serve warm.

## hot camembert pastry parcels
**Serves 2**

2 x 375g sheets ready-rolled all-butter
puff pastry
Plain flour to dust
125g camembert round
1 ready-roasted red pepper, sliced
1 tbsp thyme leaves, plus 6 extra sprigs
1 medium free-range egg, beaten

1. Preheat the oven to 200°C/fan180°C/
gas 6 and put a baking tray lined with
baking paper in the oven to heat up.
2. Put the puff pastry on a lightly floured
surface and trim each sheet with a knife
into a 20cm square.
3. Halve the camembert horizontally

through the centre to make 2 rounds.
Top the cut side of one round with the
sliced pepper, then top with the other
cheese round. Cut this in half vertically
to make 2 semicircles.
4. Put one of the semicircles slightly off
centre on top of one of the pastry
squares. Season with black pepper and
sprinkle with half the thyme leaves.
5. Brush the pastry edges with some
beaten egg, then fold them over the
cheese and press down to form a parcel.
Crimp the edges with a fork to seal.
6. Brush the parcel with the beaten egg
and top with a few thyme sprigs. Repeat
with the remaining pastry and cheese.
7. Transfer to the prepared tray, then
bake for 20-25 minutes until cooked
and golden. Slice in half and serve warm.

Thai chicken parcels

Mini pasties

## mini pasties

**Makes 36**

Allow for 3-4 small pasties per person.

300g fillet steak, trimmed and
finely chopped
1 large carrot, finely chopped
1 potato (about 275g), finely chopped
1 onion, finely chopped
1 tbsp Worcestershire sauce
2 tsp plain flour, plus extra to dust
6 x 375g sheets ready-rolled
shortcrust pastry
1 medium free-range egg, beaten
Tomato chutney (see Basics, p124)
and mixed salad leaves to serve

1. Preheat the oven to 180°C/fan160°C/
gas 4. Line 2 baking trays with baking
paper. Combine the meat, carrot, potato
and onion in a large bowl. Season, then
stir in the Worcestershire sauce. Sprinkle
over the flour and toss to coat.
2. Using a lightly floured 10cm round
cutter, cut 6 circles out of a sheet of
pastry. Spoon 1 heaped tablespoon of
the filling into the centre of each circle.
Brush the edges lightly with some of the
beaten egg. Bring up the pastry edges
and press to seal. Pinch to create a
decorative frill and put on the prepared
baking trays with the frill upright,
spaced 2cm apart. Repeat with the
remaining pastry sheets.
3. Brush the pasties with the remaining
beaten egg, then bake for 40-50 minutes
until golden and cooked through. Serve
warm or at room temperature with
tomato chutney and salad leaves.

## moussaka filo parcels

**Makes 8**

1 tbsp olive oil, plus extra for brushing
1 onion, finely chopped
2 garlic cloves, finely chopped
500g lean lamb mince
1 tbsp tomato paste
½ tsp ground cinnamon
400g tin chopped tomatoes
2 tsp dried oregano
600g aubergine, sliced into 1cm rounds

Moussaka filo parcels

150ml thick Greek-style yogurt
30g finely grated parmesan
50g feta, crumbled
8 filo pastry sheets
60g unsalted butter, melted, to brush
Green salad to serve

1. Heat the oil in a large frying pan over
a medium heat. Add the onion and garlic
and cook, stirring, for 5 minutes until
soft. Increase the heat to medium-high,
add the lamb and cook, stirring to break
it up, for 5 minutes until browned.
2. Add the tomato paste and cinnamon
and cook, stirring, for 1 minute or until
fragrant. Add the tomatoes, oregano
and 200ml water. Season with sea salt
and black pepper, then bring to a
simmer. Reduce the heat to medium-low
and simmer, uncovered, for 30 minutes,
stirring occasionally, until most of the
liquid has evaporated. Set aside to cool.
3. Meanwhile preheat a grill to medium-
high. Line 2 baking trays with lightly

oiled foil. Arrange the aubergine slices
on the trays, brush with olive oil and
season. Grill for 7-8 minutes per tray,
turning the slices, until lightly golden
and tender. Set aside to cool.
4. Preheat the oven to 220°C/fan200°C/
gas 7 and line 2 baking trays with baking
paper. Combine the yogurt, parmesan,
feta and some seasoning. Put a sheet of
filo on a work surface with the long edge
towards you (keep the other sheets
covered with a lightly dampened tea
towel). Brush with butter and top with
another sheet of filo pastry. Cut in half
widthways to form 2 rough squares.
5. Put 1 aubergine slice in the centre of
each square. Top with mince, another
piece of aubergine and 1 heaped tbsp
yogurt mix. Brush the filo edges with
butter, then bring up the sides and
scrunch into parcels. Put on the baking
tray. Repeat to make 8 parcels. Brush
with butter, then bake for 15-20 minutes
until golden. Serve with a green salad.

Party sausage rolls

## party sausage rolls
**Makes 24**

500g good-quality pork sausages, skins removed
1 small onion, finely chopped
3 sun-dried tomatoes, finely chopped
4 fresh sage leaves, finely chopped
3 tbsp finely chopped fresh flatleaf parsley
2 x 375g sheets ready-rolled all-butter puff pastry
Plain flour to dust
1 medium free-range egg, beaten
20g parmesan, finely grated

1. Preheat the oven to 200°C/fan180°C/gas 6. Line 2 baking trays with baking paper. Put the sausagemeat in a bowl with the onion, sun-dried tomatoes, sage and parsley. Season and mix well.
2. Put the pastry on a lightly floured surface and cut each sheet in half to make 4 rectangles. Roll the sausage mix into 4 x 24cm logs. Place 1 log along the long side of a pastry rectangle, 5mm in from the edge. Brush the edge with egg, then fold the pastry over the filling and press to seal. Crimp with the back of a fork. Repeat with the remaining pastry and filling, then chill for 20 minutes.
3. Trim the ends of the logs with a sharp knife, brush the pastry with beaten egg, then sprinkle with parmesan. Slice each roll into 6 and put on the baking trays. Bake for 20-25 minutes until golden and risen. Remove from the oven and cool slightly on a wire rack, then serve.

## lentil and spinach en croûte
**Serves 3-4**

100g mushrooms, sliced
1 tbsp olive oil
100g baby spinach
150g jar roasted peppers, drained and sliced
2 x 400g tins lentils, drained and rinsed
2 tsp mild curry powder
2 tbsp mango chutney, plus extra to serve
375g block all-butter puff pastry
Plain flour to dust
60g finely grated cheddar, plus extra to sprinkle
1 medium free-range egg, beaten
Greek yogurt and salad to serve

1. In a large pan, cook the mushrooms in the olive oil over a medium heat, stirring, for 1 minute. Add the spinach, peppers, lentils, curry powder and the 2 tbsp chutney, then season. Cook for 2-3 minutes, stirring, until the spinach has wilted, then leave to cool.
2. Preheat the oven to 180°C/fan160°C/gas 4. Line a tray with baking paper. Roll out the pastry on a floured surface to form a 40cm x 30cm rectangle. Spread half the lentils down the centre, top with cheese, then the rest of the lentils. Brush the pastry edges with some of the beaten egg, then fold over to enclose the filling, pressing to seal. Put on the lined tray, seam-side down.
3. Brush the top with beaten egg, then sprinkle with cheese. Bake for 30 minutes until golden. Serve with yogurt, salad and mango chutney.

Lentil and spinach
en croûte

Chocolate and vanilla
custard buns

## chocolate and vanilla custard buns
**Makes 8**

1 quantity of Danish pastry dough (see Basics, p124) or 500g block all-butter puff pastry
Plain flour to dust
1 vanilla pod, split and seeds scraped
150ml milk
1 medium free-range egg, beaten, plus 1 egg yolk
1½ tbsp caster sugar
1 tbsp cornflour
80ml double cream, whipped to soft peaks

**FOR THE CHOCOLATE ICING**
1 free-range medium egg white
150g icing sugar, sifted
2 tbsp cocoa powder
1 tsp double cream

1. Preheat the oven to 200°C/fan180°C/gas 6. Line 2 baking trays with baking paper. Roll out the pastry on a lightly floured work surface to a thickness of 5mm, then cut into 8 x 10cm squares. Make diagonal 3cm cuts from the corners of the squares into the middle. Chill while you make the filling.
2. Heat the vanilla pod, seeds and milk in a small pan over a low heat until just below boiling point.
3. Meanwhile, whisk the yolk and sugar in a bowl until pale and fluffy. Whisk in the cornflour. Gradually add the hot milk (discarding the vanilla pod) and whisk until smooth. Return the custard to a clean pan over a low heat and whisk for 4 minutes until thick enough to coat the back of a spoon. Remove from the heat and cover the surface with baking paper to stop a skin forming. Cool completely, then fold in the whipped cream.
4. To make the icing, beat the egg white until stiff. Whisk in the icing sugar, cocoa and a pinch of salt, then stir in the cream and mix until smooth.
5. To assemble the buns, spoon 1 tbsp custard into the middle of each square, then fold every second corner at right angles over the filling so they just

Festive mince wreath

overlap and form a pinwheel. Cover with cling film and chill for 20 minutes.
6. Brush with beaten egg and bake for 18-20 minutes until golden. Cool slightly, then spoon icing over the middle of each pastry and serve warm.

## festive mince wreath
**Makes 1 large wreath**

3 x 375g ready-rolled sheets all-butter puff pastry
Plain flour to dust
300g mincemeat
25g flaked almonds
Grated zest of 1 orange
Grated zest of ½ lemon
1 medium free-range egg, beaten
50g icing sugar

1. Preheat the oven to 200°C/fan180°C/gas 6. Line a large baking tray with

baking paper, then put 2 of the pastry sheets on a lightly floured surface. Spread the mincemeat, almonds and zests over the top and roll each widthways into a swiss roll shape. Brush with egg. Trim the ends and cut into 20 x 2cm thick rounds. Arrange the rounds on the baking tray in a wreath shape, pressing them together.
2. To make a bow, cut 2 x 3cm thick strips from the remaining pastry sheet. Fold one to make the loops, then use the other to form the knot. Press the bow into the base of the wreath and brush with beaten egg. Chill for 20 minutes.
3. Mix the icing sugar with 1-2 tbsp water to make a thin icing. Set aside.
4. Bake the wreath for 20-25 minutes until golden and puffed up. Cool on the tray for 10 minutes, then carefully transfer to a rack to cool completely. Drizzle over the icing and serve warm.

Pea and smoked trout tart, p91

# savoury tarts and pies

Spring herb tartlets, p91

Greek lamb pies with
feta mash topping

## greek lamb pies with feta mash topping
**Serves 4-6**

1kg lamb shoulder, cut into 2.5cm cubes
2 tbsp plain flour
3 tbsp olive oil
1 large red onion, chopped
2 garlic cloves, chopped
2 tbsp roughly chopped fresh oregano, or 2 tsp dried oregano
75g pitted kalamata olives
600ml dry red wine
300ml beef stock
Grated zest and juice of ½ lemon
Large bunch of fresh mint, chopped

FOR THE MASH TOPPING
1kg floury potatoes, cubed
250ml milk, heated
50g butter, melted
180g feta, drained, crumbled

1. Preheat the oven to 160°C/fan140°C/gas 3. Put the lamb in a bowl with the flour, season and toss well.
2. Heat 2 tbsp oil in a large flameproof casserole over a medium heat. Fry the lamb in batches until just golden. Remove with a slotted spoon. Set aside.
3. Heat the remaining 1 tbsp oil in the casserole, add the onion and cook for 2-3 minutes until soft. Stir in the garlic, oregano and olives. Turn the heat to high, add the wine and boil rapidly for 3-4 minutes. Add the stock and lamb, then season and bring to the boil.
4. Cover and bake for 1½ hours until the lamb is tender and the sauce has thickened. Set aside to cool. Turn up the oven to 200°C/fan180°C/gas 6.
5. Meanwhile, for the topping, boil the potatoes in a pan of salted water for 15-20 minutes. Drain, then pass through a potato ricer or mash until smooth. Return to the pan and beat in the milk and butter. Stir in 120g feta and season.
6. Stir the lemon zest and juice and the mint into the lamb. Divide among 4 x 500ml (or 6 x 350ml) pie dishes. Spoon the mash on top and sprinkle with the remaining feta. Bake the pies for 30-35 minutes until golden, then serve.

## spring herb tartlets
**Serves 4**

1 medium free-range egg, plus 2 yolks, lightly beaten
125ml double cream
Handful of fresh mint leaves, chopped
Handful of fresh flatleaf parsley, chopped
Handful of fresh chives, chopped
75g mature cheddar, finely grated
Freshly grated nutmeg
Tomato chutney (see Basics, p124) to serve

FOR THE WALNUT PASTRY
50g walnuts
220g plain flour, plus extra to dust
½ tsp salt
125g cold unsalted butter, cubed
About 3 tbsp iced water

1. For the pastry, whizz the nuts in a food processor until finely chopped. Sift the flour and salt into a large bowl, then add the nuts and butter. Rub in with your fingers until the mixture resembles fine crumbs. Pour over the iced water, then mix with a knife until the pastry starts to come together, adding more water if necessary. Knead briefly, shape into a disc, then wrap in cling film and chill for 30 minutes.
2. Roll out the pastry on a floured surface until 5mm thick. Cut 4 x 15cm discs and use to line 4 x 10cm loose-bottomed fluted tart tins. Trim any excess, prick the bases all over with a fork, then chill for 30 minutes.
3. Preheat the oven to 220°C/fan200°C/gas 7. Put the tart cases on a baking tray and line with baking paper and baking beans or rice. Blind bake for 12-15 minutes until crisp. Remove from the oven, remove the beans/rice and paper, then set aside to cool slightly.
4. Turn down the oven to 180°C/fan160°C/gas 4. Mix the eggs and yolks in a bowl with the cream, herbs and cheese. Add a grating of nutmeg and season well.
5. Fill the tart cases with the egg mixture, then bake for 20-25 minutes until golden and just set. Serve warm with tomato chutney.

## pea and smoked trout tart
**Serves 4**

375g block all-butter puff pastry
180g frozen peas
480g ricotta
Grated zest of 1 lemon, plus 1 tbsp juice
2 tbsp olive oil
200g smoked trout
25g pea shoots

1. Preheat the oven to 180°C/fan160°C/gas 4. Line a large baking tray with baking paper.
2. Roll out the pastry on a lightly floured surface to a 16cm x 30cm rectangle. Put on the tray, then bake for 10 minutes or until the pastry is puffed. Top with more paper and another baking tray, then bake for a further 10 minutes or until golden and crisp. Allow to cool.
3. Meanwhile, cook the peas for 2-3 minutes in salted boiling water until tender. Refresh in cold water, drain, then whizz in a food processor with the ricotta and lemon zest to make a chunky purée. Season.
4. In a small bowl, whisk the oil with the lemon juice and some seasoning. When ready to serve, spread the pea and ricotta mixture over the pastry, flake over the smoked trout, then scatter with the pea shoots. Drizzle the dressing over the tart and serve immediately.

Antipasti tart

## russian fish pie
**Serves 6-8**

65g basmati rice
20g unsalted butter
1 tbsp olive oil
1 large onion, finely chopped
150g chestnut mushrooms, chopped
1 tsp ground turmeric
Handful of chopped fresh dill
Handful of chopped fresh flatleaf parsley
1 tbsp capers, rinsed and chopped
Finely grated zest of 1 lemon
2 hard-boiled eggs, chopped,
plus 1 beaten egg to brush
Plain flour for dusting
2 x 375g blocks all-butter puff pastry
800g skinless salmon fillet, pin-boned

1. Preheat the oven to 200°C/fan180°C/
gas 6. Line a baking tray with baking
paper. Cook the rice according to the
packet instructions, then cool completely.
2. Meanwhile, heat the butter and oil
in a pan over a low heat. Add the onion
and cook, stirring, for 5-6 minutes until
softened. Add the mushrooms and cook
for 5-8 minutes until tender. Stir in the
turmeric and toss to coat, then stir in
the rice, herbs, capers, lemon zest and
chopped eggs. Season and allow to cool.
3. On a floured surface, roll out one of
the blocks of pastry to 5mm thick. Trim
to a 30cm x 20cm rectangle. Put on
the prepared tray, then put the salmon
on top in the centre. Season, then top
the salmon with the rice mixture. Brush
the pastry edges with beaten egg, then
roll out the second block of pastry to
cover the filling and put on top. Trim,
leaving a 2cm border, then press down
the edges to seal. Use the trimmings
to decorate the top, if you like.
4. Bake for 35-40 minutes until golden
and cooked through. Serve warm.

## antipasti tart
**Serves 4-6**

375g block all-butter puff pastry
Plain flour for dusting
3 tbsp sun-blush tomato pesto
125g cherry tomatoes, halved
150g mixed antipasti
100g feta, crumbled
Small fresh basil leaves to serve

1. Preheat the oven to 200°C/fan180°C/
gas 6. Line a baking tray with baking
paper. Roll out the puff pastry on
a dusted surface to form a rectangle,
5mm thick. Put on the baking tray.
2. Score a 2.5cm border around the edge
of the pastry and prick the base all over
with a fork. Spread the tomato pesto
over the pastry inside the border, then
top with the tomatoes, antipasti and feta.
3. Bake for 15-20 minutes until the
pastry is golden and crisp. Sprinkle
with the basil leaves, then serve.

Russian fish pie

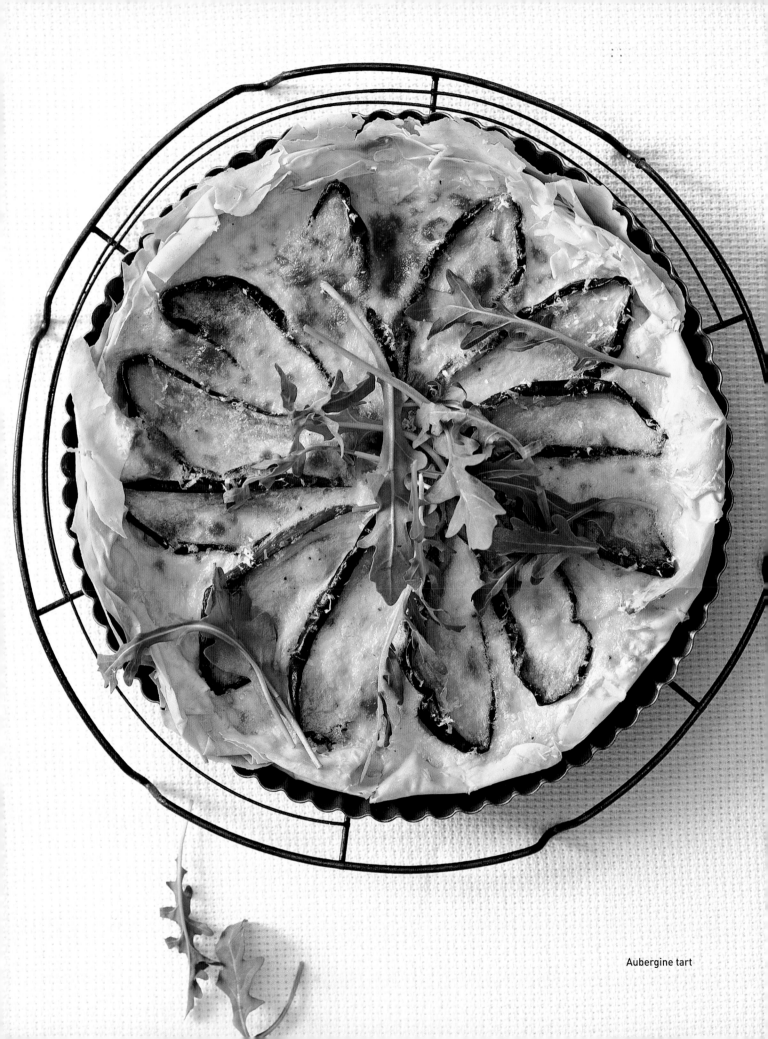

Aubergine tart

Spinach and feta filo pie

## aubergine tart
**Serves 4-6**

2 tbsp olive oil, plus extra for greasing
6 baby aubergines, trimmed and halved lengthways
4 filo pastry sheets, halved lengthways
160g finely grated parmesan
2 large free-range eggs
175ml double cream
Rocket leaves to garnish

1. Preheat the oven to 180°C/fan160°C/gas 4 and line a baking tray with baking paper. Grease a deep 22cm loose-bottomed fluted flan case.
2. Brush 1 tbsp oil over the aubergine halves and place, cut-side down, in a single layer on the baking tray. Season, then bake for 25 minutes or until tender when pierced with a sharp knife.
3. Brush one pastry sheet with olive oil and use to line the tart tin. Repeat with the remaining filo sheets, giving the tin a quarter turn each time. Sprinkle half the cheese over the pastry, then arrange the aubergines in a circle on top.
4. Beat the eggs and cream together. Season, then pour into the tart tin. Fold over the edges of the pastry, then sprinkle the remaining cheese over the top and bake the tart for 20 minutes or until golden and set. Allow to cool for 10 minutes, then serve warm or at room temperature, garnished with rocket.

## spinach and feta filo pie
**Serves 4**

500g baby leaf spinach
50g unsalted butter
1 onion, finely chopped
2 garlic cloves, finely chopped
200g feta, crumbled
50g toasted pine nuts
3 medium free-range eggs, beaten
12 filo pastry sheets
½ tsp caraway seeds

1. Put the spinach in a large pan over a low heat for 2-3 minutes until wilted. Cool, then drain and squeeze out the excess liquid.
2. Melt 20g of the butter in a pan over a medium-low heat. Add the onion and cook, stirring, for 5-6 minutes until soft. Stir in the garlic and cook for 1 minute.
3. Remove from the heat and put in a bowl with the spinach, feta, pine nuts and eggs. Mix together and season, then spoon into a 1 litre baking dish.
4. Preheat the oven to 180°C/fan160°C/gas 4. Melt the remaining butter, then brush 1 filo pastry sheet with butter, lightly scrunch and place over the spinach mixture. Repeat with the rest of the pastry sheets until the filling is completely covered. Brush the top with any remaining butter.
5. Sprinkle with caraway seeds, then bake for 25-30 minutes until the pastry is crisp and golden. Serve warm.

Tomato
tarte tatin

## tomato tarte tatin
**Serves 4**
To get the correct results here,
make sure it's the top of the pan
that measures 24cm.

350g cherry tomatoes
Handful of fresh thyme sprigs, leaves
picked, plus extra sprigs to serve
1 tbsp balsamic vinegar
375g block all-butter puff pastry
20g parmesan, finely grated

1. Preheat the oven to 200°C/fan180°C/
gas 6. Mix the tomatoes with the thyme
leaves, then spread evenly in a 24cm
heavy-based ovenproof frying pan.
Drizzle with the balsamic vinegar.
2. Roll out the pastry on a lightly floured
surface to a 30cm square, then cut out
a rough circle a little wider than the top
of the pan. Discard the leftover pastry.
3. Sprinkle half the parmesan over the
tomatoes, then top with the pastry,
tucking the edges in well.
4. Sprinkle with the remaining cheese,
then bake for 30-35 minutes until the
pastry is crisp and dry.
5. Allow the tart to stand for 2 minutes
before turning out onto a serving plate.
Sprinkle with the extra thyme sprigs
and serve warm.

## chinese-spiced beef pie
**Serves 6**
This is perfect served with steamed
or stir-fried Chinese greens. Make
the filling the day before to allow the
flavours to develop fully.

2 tbsp sunflower oil
1 large onion, finely chopped
3 garlic cloves, finely chopped
1kg good-quality stewing beef
(such as chuck steak)
1½ tbsp sichuan peppercorns
(from large supermarkets and Asian
grocers)
25g plain flour
4 potatoes, cut into large cubes
4 star anise
1 cinnamon stick
4cm fresh ginger, finely chopped
100ml light soy sauce
80ml dark soy sauce
3 large red chillies
2 tbsp dark brown muscovado sugar

**FOR THE PASTRY**
300g plain flour
100g cold butter, cubed
A few tbsp iced water
1 medium free-range egg, beaten,
to glaze
2 tsp sesame seeds

1. Heat 1 tbsp oil in a large flameproof
casserole over a medium heat. Add
the onion and garlic, then cook for 2
minutes until starting to soften. Remove
with a slotted spoon and set aside.
Increase the heat to medium-high and
add the remaining oil to the casserole.
Brown the meat, in batches, for
2 minutes, then remove and set aside.
2. Finely crush the peppercorns in a
pestle and mortar, then add the flour.
Cook the spiced flour in the casserole
for 5 seconds over a high heat. Return
the meat and onions to the dish and
toss everything together.
3. Add the remaining ingredients and
cover with 400ml water. Bring to a
simmer, then cook, covered, over a very
low heat for 1½ hours until the meat is
tender and the sauce is thick and glossy.
Remove from the heat and leave to cool.
4. Meanwhile make the pastry. Mix the
flour with a good pinch of salt in a bowl,
then add the butter. Use your fingertips
to rub the butter into the flour until the
mixture resembles fine crumbs. Slowly
add iced water, 1 tbsp at a time, stirring
with a round-bladed knife, until the
dough just sticks together. Turn out onto
a lightly floured surface and knead
lightly into a ball. Wrap in cling film,
then chill for at least 15 minutes.
5. Preheat the oven to 200°C/fan180°C/
gas 6. Transfer the cooled filling to
a 2 litre pie dish. Roll out the pastry on
a lightly floured surface to a round that's
2.5cm larger than the dish. Put a pie
funnel in the centre of the filling,
moisten the edges of the dish with a
little beaten egg, then put the pastry on
top, pressing down on the edges to seal.
6. Trim the excess pastry, then crimp
the edges with a fork or between your
thumb and forefinger. Brush the pastry
with beaten egg and sprinkle with
sesame seeds. Make a hole in the centre
of the lid to reveal the pie funnel. Bake
for 35-40 minutes until crisp, golden
and piping hot. Cool slightly, then serve.

Chinese-spiced beef pie

Sausage and chard pie

## sausage and chard pie
**Serves 4**

400g good-quality pork and leek
sausages
25g unsalted butter
1 onion, thinly sliced
1 tbsp plain flour
175ml chicken stock
300g chard, thick central rib removed,
leaves torn
Juice of ½ lemon
375g block all-butter puff pastry
1 medium free-range egg, lightly beaten
Tomato chutney (see Basics, p124)
to serve

1. Heat a griddle or frying pan over
a low-medium heat. Cook the sausages,
turning often, for 10-12 minutes until
just cooked. Remove and set aside.
2. Melt the butter in a frying pan over a
low-medium heat, add the onion and
cook, stirring, for 8-10 minutes until
soft. Add the flour and cook, stirring,
for 1 minute. Take off the heat and
gradually add the stock, stirring, until
the sauce is smooth and thick. Return
to the heat and simmer for 1 minute.
3. In a colander over the sink, pour
boiling water over the chard. Once
wilted, rinse under cold water. Squeeze
out any excess liquid, roughly chop
and put in a bowl.
4. Cut the sausage into chunks, then
stir into the sauce. Add the lemon juice
and some seasoning, then leave to cool.
Put in a 1.2 litre pie dish.
5. Roll out the pastry on a lightly floured
surface to about 5mm thick. Brush the
edges of the pie dish with some of the
beaten egg, then cover with the pastry.
Trim any excess, then press to seal.
6. Cut a cross in the centre to let steam
escape, then chill for 20 minutes.
7. Preheat the oven to 200°C/fan180°C/
gas 6. Brush with beaten egg, then bake
for 15-20 minutes. Reduce the heat to
180°C/fan160°C/gas 4, then bake for
15 minutes more until golden. Serve
warm with some tomato chutney.

Chicken, leek
and gruyère tart

## chicken, leek and gruyère tart
**Serves 4**

1 quantity shortcrust pastry (see
Basics, p124) or 375g pack ready-rolled
shortcrust pastry
Plain flour to dust
1 tbsp olive oil
30g butter
2 large leeks, sliced
3 fresh thyme sprigs
2 tbsp wholegrain mustard
150g shredded, cooked chicken
3 medium free-range eggs, lightly beaten
300ml double cream
50g gruyère, grated

1. Preheat the oven to 200°C/fan180°C/
gas 6. Roll out the pastry on a lightly
floured surface to a 28cm round. Press
into a 23cm loose-bottomed tart tin,
allowing pastry to drape over the edges.
Trim the excess pastry, then prick the
base all over with a fork. Chill for
10 minutes. Line the pastry case with
baking paper, fill with baking beans or
rice, then blind bake for 10 minutes.
2. Remove the paper and beans/rice,
then blind bake for a further 5 minutes
until crisp. Turn down the oven
temperature to 180°C/fan160°C/gas 4.
3. Meanwhile heat the oil and butter in
a pan over a low-medium heat. Add the
leeks and thyme, then cook, stirring, for
5 minutes or until the leeks are tender.
4. Spread the mustard over the base of
the tart, then top with the leeks. Scatter
the shredded chicken over the top.
5. In a bowl, mix the eggs, cream and
gruyère. Season well, then pour into the
tart case. Bake for 25-30 minutes until
set and golden. Cool slightly, then
remove from the tin. Serve warm.

## beef and ale raised pies

**Makes 6**

2 tbsp olive oil, plus extra to grease
2 onions, finely chopped
3 garlic cloves, finely chopped
800g trimmed chuck steak,
cut into 2cm cubes
2 tbsp plain flour, seasoned
3 fresh thyme sprigs
1 bay leaf
350ml dark ale
250ml beef stock
2 tsp English mustard
2 tbsp Worcestershire sauce

**FOR THE HOT WATER PASTRY**
80g unsalted butter, cubed
80g lard, chopped
450g plain flour, plus extra for dusting
1 tsp salt
3 medium free-range eggs

1. To make the pastry, put the butter and lard in a pan with 150ml water. Bring to the boil, stirring, until the lard and the butter have melted. Meanwhile, sift the flour and salt into a bowl. Make a well in the centre. Lightly beat 2 of the eggs and add to the well, then cover them up with the flour. Pour the just-boiled butter and water mixture around the edge of the flour, then mix quickly with a wooden spoon until combined and smooth. Tip onto a lightly floured surface, knead for 1 minute, then wrap in cling film and refrigerate for 1 hour.

2. Meanwhile, heat 1 tbsp of the oil in a large pan over a low-medium heat and cook the onions and garlic for 10 minutes until soft but not coloured. Remove with a slotted spoon and set aside.

3. Put the steak in a bowl with the 2 tbsp flour and toss to coat. Heat half the remaining oil in the pan, add half the beef and cook, turning, for 5-6 minutes until browned all over. Repeat with the rest of the oil and the remaining beef.

4. Return the onions and garlic to the pan with all the beef. Add the rest of the filling ingredients, then stir to combine. Bring to the boil, then cover and simmer over a low heat for 2 hours until the meat is tender.

5. Discard the bay leaves and thyme sprigs. Season, then transfer the pie filling to a bowl to cool completely.

6. Preheat the oven to 200°C/fan180°C/ gas 6. Reserve one-third of the pastry for lids, re-wrap in cling film and refrigerate until needed.

7. Divide the remaining pastry into 6 equal pieces. Roll out the pastry on a lightly floured surface to 17cm circles. Lightly oil 6 x 250ml metal pudding basins. Line each one with a pastry circle, using your fingers to press it evenly around the sides and to work the pastry up over the edge. Chill uncovered in the fridge for 40 minutes to firm up.

8. Divide the cooled filling among the cases. Divide the reserved pastry into 6 equal portions. Roll out each piece to a circle large enough to make a lid.

9. Lightly beat the remaining egg, make a hole in the centre of each lid and dampen the edges of the pastry with beaten egg. Put the pastry circles over the cases, then pinch to seal. Brush the tops with the rest of the beaten egg.

10. Bake in the oven for 40 minutes (covering with foil if the pastry browns too quickly) until the pastry is golden and crisp and the filling is piping hot. Allow the pies to rest for 5 minutes, then carefully remove them from the pie moulds and serve hot.

Beef and ale raised pies

Mango tartes tatins, p105

# sweet tarts and pies

Rich almond tart
with drunken
strawberries, p105

Late-summer
apple pie

## late-summer apple pie
**Serves 8-10**

1.5kg (about 9) bramley apples
150g light muscovado sugar
or light brown sugar
1 tsp ground cinnamon
½ tsp freshly grated nutmeg
Icing sugar to dust
Whipped double cream or
ice cream to serve

**FOR THE PASTRY**
350g plain flour, plus extra to dust
175g chilled unsalted butter, chopped,
plus extra for greasing
50g caster sugar
1 medium free-range egg, lightly beaten
1-2 tbsp cold milk (optional),
plus extra to brush

1. For the pastry, put the flour, butter
and caster sugar in a food processor
and whizz until the mixture resembles
breadcrumbs.
2. Add the egg and pulse until the pastry
comes together. (You may need to add
a little milk if the mixture is too dry.)
Wrap in cling film, then chill for 1 hour.
3. Meanwhile, peel, core and cut the
apples into 1cm thick slices. Put in
a pan with the muscovado or brown
sugar, the spices and 1 tbsp cold water.
Stir over a low heat to dissolve the
sugar, then cover and cook for
4-5 minutes until the apples start
to soften. Set aside to cool.
4. Grease a deep, 22cm loose-bottomed
fluted flan tin. On a lightly floured
surface, roll out two-thirds of the pastry
to make a 5mm thick disc, then use to
line the tin. Prick the base all over with
a fork, then chill for 30 minutes.
5. Roll out the remaining pastry into
a 24cm disc (this will be the pastry
lid). Wrap the pastry in cling film,
then chill until ready to use.
6. Preheat the oven to 180°C/fan160°C/
gas 4. Line the tart case with baking
paper and fill with baking beans or rice,
then blind bake for 15 minutes.
7. Remove the baking beans/rice and
baking paper, then bake for 3-5 minutes

more until the case is golden and dry.
8. Using a slotted spoon, fill the tart
case with the cooled apple mixture, then
top with the pastry lid. Trim any excess
pastry and pinch the edges together. Cut
a cross in the centre of the lid to let the
steam to escape. Brush with milk, then
bake for 30-35 minutes until golden.
9. Allow the pie to cool in the tin.
Transfer to a serving plate, then dust
with icing sugar. Serve warm or cold
with double cream or ice cream.

## rich almond tart with drunken strawberries
**Serves 8-10**
The beauty of this tart is that there's no
pastry to make, which means it's really
simple to put together, yet impressive.

500g strawberries, hulled and halved
2 tbsp strawberry liqueur or
Grand Marnier
220g caster sugar
7 medium free-range egg yolks
¾ tsp almond essence
1½ tsp vanilla extract
50g plain flour
200g ground almonds
225g chilled unsalted butter, diced, plus
extra to grease
Whipped double cream to serve

1. Put the berries in a bowl and sprinkle
with the liqueur and 2 tbsp of the sugar.
Stir very gently, then cover and chill,
stirring occasionally, for 1-2 hours.
2. In another bowl, whisk 6 egg yolks
with the almond essence and vanilla.
3. Put the flour, ground almonds and
the remaining caster sugar in a food
processor, then whizz until combined.
With the motor running, pour in the yolk
mixture and whizz until it starts to form
a paste. Add the butter and whizz again,
scraping down the sides occasionally,
until thick, smooth and creamy. (Don't
over-process.)
4. Preheat the oven to 190°C/170°C/
gas 5. Grease a 25cm loose-bottomed
fluted flan tin and line the base with
greased baking paper.
5. Spoon the mixture into the tart tin and

level the surface with a palette knife.
Refrigerate for 10-15 minutes until
slightly firm. Beat the remaining egg
yolk and brush over the chilled tart.
Chill for a further 5 minutes.
6. Use a fork to trace a wavy pattern
on the top of the tart. Put on a baking
sheet and bake for 12 minutes.
7. Reduce the oven temperature to
160°C/fan140°C/gas 3. Bake for a
further 30 minutes until golden and
just set on top when lightly pressed.
8. Cool the tart in the tin on a wire
rack for 15 minutes, then remove
from the tin and allow to cool on its
paper on a rack. Serve with whipped
cream and the drunken strawberries.

## mango tartes tatins
**Makes 4**

2 x 320g sheets ready-rolled puff pastry
165g caster sugar
1 vanilla pod, split, seeds scraped
50g unsalted butter, chopped,
plus extra to grease
4 mangoes, stoned and thinly sliced
Coconut or vanilla ice cream to serve

1. Preheat the oven to 180°C/fan160°C/
gas 4. Grease 4 x 11cm pie or tart tins
(not loose-bottomed). Using an inverted
tin as a guide, cut 4 discs from the
pastry. Chill the discs for 15 minutes.
2. Put the sugar and vanilla seeds
in a saucepan with 2 tbsp water, stirring
over a low heat until the sugar has
dissolved. Increase the heat to medium
and cook for 5-6 minutes to give a
golden caramel, swirling the pan
occasionally and brushing down the
sides with a damp pastry brush to
prevent crystals forming. Divide the
caramel among the tart tins. Cool
slightly, then dot with the butter.
3. Arrange overlapping slices of mango
over the caramel. Cover with the pastry
rounds, tucking in the edges. Put the
tarts on a baking tray and bake for 20
minutes or until the pastry is puffed and
golden. Cool in the tins for 5 minutes.
4. Carefully invert the tarts onto plates
and serve topped with ice cream.

Vanilla tart with poached apricots

## raspberry shortcakes with basil cream

**Makes 4**

Make crystallised basil by lightly brushing small basil leaves with beaten egg white. Dip in caster sugar to coat, then chill on a tray for 15 minutes.

200g good-quality shortbread
50g unsalted butter, melted, plus extra for greasing
250g raspberries
1 tbsp icing sugar
2 small passion fruit
300ml double cream
60g crème fraîche
2 tbsp thick Greek-style yogurt
6 basil leaves, plus 4 small crystallised leaves (optional) to serve

1. Preheat the oven to 170°C/fan150°C/ gas 3½. Grease 4 x 10cm loose-bottomed fluted flan tins.
2. Whizz the biscuits to fine crumbs in a food processor. Add the melted butter and whizz to combine. Press the mixture into the base and up the sides of the tart tins. Put the tins on a baking tray, then bake for 5-10 minutes or until firm and lightly golden. Allow to cool, then chill while you make the filling.
3. Purée half the raspberries with the icing sugar in a blender or food processor. Press through a sieve into a bowl, discarding the seeds, then chill.
4. Scoop the seeds and pulp from the passion fruit into a sieve over a bowl. Press the passion fruit juices through the sieve. Discard the seeds. Beat the cream to soft peaks. Stir in the crème fraîche, yogurt and passion fruit juices. Finely chop the 6 basil leaves, then fold into the cream mixture.
5. Remove the tarts from the tins. Fill the tart cases with the cream mixture. Top with the remaining berries, then drizzle with the raspberry sauce. Garnish with crystallised basil leaves, if you like. Any leftover raspberry sauce can be kept, covered, for up to a week in the fridge – it's great with ice cream.

## vanilla tart with poached apricots

**Serves 8**

200g plain flour, plus extra to dust
100g chilled unsalted butter, diced
25g icing sugar, plus extra to dust
2 medium free-range eggs,
plus 2 egg yolks
2-3 tbsp iced water
400ml double cream
1 vanilla pod, split, seeds scraped
75g caster sugar

**FOR THE POACHED APRICOTS**
110g caster sugar
1 vanilla pod, split, seeds scraped
12 apricots, halved

1. Sift the flour and a pinch of salt into a bowl, then add the butter. Using your fingertips, rub the butter into the flour until it resembles breadcrumbs.
2. Stir in the icing sugar, 1 egg yolk and some iced water, then knead to combine into a soft pastry. Shape into a disc, wrap in cling film and chill for 30 minutes.
3. On a floured surface, roll out the pastry until 5mm thick and use to line a 24cm fluted, loose-bottomed tart tin. Prick the base all over with a fork and chill for 30 minutes.
4. Preheat the oven to 200°C/fan180°C/ gas 6. Line the pastry with baking paper and fill with baking beans or rice, then blind bake for 15 minutes. Remove the paper and beans/rice, then bake for 8-10 minutes more until dry and golden. Set aside to cool. Reduce the oven temperature to 150°C/fan130°C/gas 2.
5. Meanwhile, to make the filling, pour the cream into a saucepan. Add the vanilla pod and seeds, then bring to the boil over a medium-high heat. Remove the pan from the heat and leave the vanilla pod to infuse in the cream until cool, then remove the pod and discard.
6. Beat the eggs, remaining egg yolk, caster sugar and cooled cream together in a bowl, then pour into the pastry case. Bake for 30-35 minutes until just set. Allow to cool completely (the filling will continue to firm up as it cools).
7. Meanwhile, for the poached apricots, put the sugar, vanilla pod and seeds in a saucepan with 750ml cold water. Place over a low heat, stirring until the sugar has dissolved. Add the apricots and simmer for 5 minutes until tender.
8. Remove the apricots with a slotted spoon and set aside in a bowl. Boil the syrup over a medium heat for 10 minutes or until reduced by half and thickened slightly. Pour the syrup over the apricots, then cool completely.
9. Dust the cooled vanilla tart with icing sugar, then slice into wedges and serve with the poached apricots.

Raspberry shortcakes
with basil cream

Lemon meringue pies
with a hint of orange

## lemon meringue pies with a hint of orange
**Makes 6**

250g plain flour, plus extra for dusting
40g icing sugar
175g chilled unsalted butter, chopped
4 medium free-range egg whites,
plus 1 egg yolk
3-4 tbsp iced water
220g caster sugar

**FOR THE FILLING**
400ml lemon juice (about 8-10 lemons)
Finely grated zest of 1 orange
75g cornflour, sifted
4 medium free-range egg yolks
250g caster sugar

1. Sift the flour and icing sugar into a bowl with a pinch of salt. Rub the butter into the mixture with your fingertips until it resembles crumbs (or pulse in a food processor). Add the egg yolk and 3-4 tbsp iced water to bring the mixture together with a knife.
2. Knead briefly on a lightly floured surface, then shape into a disc, wrap in cling film and chill for 30 minutes.
3. Divide the pastry into 6 equal pieces, then roll out on a floured surface to 5mm thick. Use to line 6 x 10cm loose-bottomed fluted tart tins. Place on a baking sheet, line each tart with baking paper, then fill with baking beans or rice. Chill for 30 minutes.
4. Preheat the oven to 200°C/fan180°C/gas 6. Blind bake the tarts for 10-12 minutes. Remove the paper and beans/rice, then blind bake the tarts for 4-5 minutes more until dry and crisp. Turn down the oven to 150°C/fan130°C/gas 2.
5. For the filling, put the lemon juice and orange zest into a pan. Whisk in the cornflour, add 250ml water, then bring to the boil over a medium-high heat. Reduce to a simmer, whisking constantly, for 3 minutes until thick. Remove from the heat and whisk in the yolks and the 250g caster sugar, then return to a low heat and simmer for 2 minutes. Cool, then pour into the cases.

Freeform blackberry and apple pie

6. Whisk the egg whites in a clean, dry bowl to stiff peaks. Whisk in the 220g caster sugar, 1 tbsp at a time, until the meringue is stiff and glossy. Spoon onto the tarts and bake for 15-20 minutes until golden. Serve the pies warm or at room temperature.

## freeform blackberry and apple pie
**Serves 6**

200g plain flour
125g chilled unsalted butter, chopped
1 medium free-range egg, lightly beaten
110g caster sugar
3 granny smith apples, cut into slices
300g blackberries
Finely grated zest of 1 lemon,
plus 1 tbsp lemon juice
25g fresh breadcrumbs
Warm custard (see Basics, p124) to serve

1. Whizz the flour and butter in a food processor until the mixture resembles breadcrumbs. Add the egg and 2 tbsp of the sugar, then whizz until the mixture just forms a ball. Shape into a disc, wrap in cling film, then chill for 30 minutes.
2. Preheat the oven to 200°C/fan180°C/gas 6. Put the apples in a bowl with the berries, zest and juice, and all but 1 tbsp of the remaining sugar. Set aside.
3. Roll out the pastry on a sheet of lightly floured baking paper to a 30cm disc. Transfer to a greased baking tray.
4. Sprinkle the pastry with breadcrumbs, leaving an 8cm border, top with the fruit, then fold the pastry border up and over the filling to partially cover. Sprinkle the pastry with the remaining sugar, then bake for 35-40 minutes until the pastry is golden and the fruit is tender. Serve the pie warm with custard.

**sweet tarts and pies.**

Frangipane apple tart with apricot glaze

## chocolate and peanut butter swirl tart
**Serves 10-12**

200g plain flour, plus extra to dust
80g unsalted butter
40g caster sugar
1 medium free-range egg yolk
1-2 tbsp iced water

**FOR THE FILLING**
200ml double cream
250g dark chocolate, chopped
1 tbsp golden syrup
50g unsalted butter
2 medium free-range eggs,
plus 1 yolk, beaten
100g white chocolate
95g smooth peanut butter

1. Sift the flour into a bowl and rub in the butter using your fingertips until it resembles crumbs (or pulse in a food processor). Stir in the sugar and a pinch of salt. Add the egg yolk and the iced water. Bring it together with a knife (or pulse). Knead into a disc, wrap in cling film, then chill for 30 minutes.
2. Roll out the pastry on a floured surface to 5mm thick, then line a 20cm fluted, loose-bottomed tart tin. Trim, prick the base all over with a fork, then chill for 30 minutes.
3. Preheat the oven to 200°C/fan180°C/ gas 6. Line the pastry with baking paper and baking beans or rice, then bake for 12 minutes. Remove the paper and beans/rice, then blind bake for 5 minutes until golden. Set aside to cool. Turn down the oven to 160°C/fan140°C/gas 3.
4. Put the cream, chocolate, syrup and butter in a heatproof bowl set over a pan of simmering water. Stir until smooth. Cool, then beat in the eggs.
5. In another heatproof bowl set over a pan of simmering water, melt the white chocolate and peanut butter together.
6. Spread two-thirds of the peanut butter mix over the pastry. Pour over the dark chocolate mixture. Spoon over the remaining peanut chocolate, then use a skewer to swirl. Bake for 25-30 minutes until set. Cool in the tin, slice and serve.

## frangipane apple tart with apricot glaze
**Serves 8**

80g unsalted butter, plus extra to grease
75g icing sugar, sifted
200g plain flour
1 medium free-range egg, lightly beaten
1 tbsp lemon juice
3 granny smith apples, peeled, thinly sliced
80g apricot jam, warmed, plus extra for brushing

**FOR THE FRANGIPANE FILLING**
100g ground almonds
100g icing sugar, sifted
1 tbsp plain flour
100g unsalted butter
2 medium free-range eggs

1. For the pastry, put the butter and icing sugar in a large bowl, then beat with an electric hand mixer until pale and fluffy.
2. Add the flour, then beat until the mixture resembles breadcrumbs.
3. In a separate small bowl, mix the beaten egg and lemon juice. Add half to the flour, then stir to form a soft dough. Add more egg mixture if the pastry is too dry. Shape the pastry into a disc, wrap in cling film, then chill for 1 hour.
4. Preheat the oven to 180°C/fan160°C/ gas 4. Roll out the pastry between 2 sheets of baking paper until 5mm thick, then use to line a greased 25cm tart tin. Chill for 15 minutes.
5. Meanwhile, for the frangipane, sift together the ground almonds, icing sugar and flour. In a large bowl, beat the 100g butter with an electric hand mixer until pale. Add the eggs, one at a time, beating well after each addition. Fold in the almond mixture.
6. Fill the tart with the frangipane, top with the apple slices, then bake for 25 minutes. Brush with the warmed jam, then return to the oven for 25 minutes until golden and set. Brush the tart with extra jam, then slice and serve.

Chocolate and peanut
butter swirl tart

Champion bakewell tart

## champion bakewell tart
**Serves 8**

200g plain flour, plus extra to dust
2 tbsp icing sugar
100g chilled unsalted butter, chopped
1 medium free-range egg,
lightly beaten

**FOR THE FILLING**
150g unsalted butter, softened
150g caster sugar
3 eggs, at room temperature, beaten
150g ground almonds
Finely grated zest of 1 lemon
110g strawberry jam
2 tbsp flaked almonds

1. Sift the flour, icing sugar and a pinch of salt into a large bowl. Using your fingertips, rub in the butter until it resembles fine crumbs. Add the beaten egg and stir with a palette knife until the pastry just comes together. Shape into a disc, wrap in cling film and chill in the fridge for 30 minutes.
2. Preheat the oven to 180°C/fan160°C/gas 4. Roll out the pastry on a floured surface until 5mm thick, then line a 24cm fluted, loose-bottomed tart tin. Trim any excess and prick the base all over with a fork. Chill for 30 minutes.
3. Line the pastry with baking paper and fill with baking beans or rice. Blind bake for 15 minutes. Remove the paper and beans/rice, then blind bake for another 5 minutes until golden and dry. Remove from the oven and set aside to cool.
4. Meanwhile, for the filling, use an electric hand mixer to beat the butter and sugar together in a bowl until pale and fluffy. Add the eggs, in 3 batches, beating well after each addition, then fold in the ground almonds and zest.
5. Spread the jam over the base of the pastry case, then spoon over the filling. Level the top with the back of the spoon.
6. Scatter over the almonds, then bake for 35-40 minutes until golden, risen and just set in the centre. Cool in the tin for 5 minutes, then transfer to a wire rack to cool completely. Slice and serve.

Macadamia tarts

## macadamia tarts
**Makes 6**

Butter for greasing
3 x 320g sheets ready-rolled shortcrust pastry
3 medium free-range eggs
180g light muscovado sugar
1 tsp vanilla extract
80ml maple syrup
60g unsalted butter, melted, cooled
225g macadamia nuts
Icing sugar to dust
Whipped double cream to serve

1. Preheat the oven to 180°C/fan160°C/gas 4. Grease 6 x 10cm fluted, loose-bottomed tartlet tins, then use the shortcrust pastry to line the tins, pressing it into the base and sides.
2. Prick the bases all over with a fork, then chill in the fridge for 15 minutes.
3. Line the tart cases with baking paper, then fill with baking beans or rice. Blind bake in the oven for 15 minutes, then remove the paper and beans/rice and bake for a further 5 minutes until the bases are dry and crisp.
4. Meanwhile, whisk the eggs, muscovado sugar, vanilla, syrup and butter together in a bowl. Pour into the tart shells.
5. Divide the macadamias evenly among the shells, then return to the oven and bake for 25 minutes until the tarts are golden and the centre is firm to touch.
6. Cool in the tins for 10 minutes, then remove from the tins, dust with icing sugar and serve with whipped cream.

Festive
slices, p117

# slices and tray bakes

Berry and apple
tray bake, p117

Apricot Danish slices

## apricot danish slices
**Serves 6-8**

Butter for greasing
180g marzipan, grated
80g full-fat cream cheese, softened
40g icing sugar, sifted, plus extra
to dust
1 tsp vanilla extract
1 medium free-range egg, beaten
Plain flour for dusting
375g block all-butter puff pastry
100g apricot jam
50g flaked almonds

1. Preheat the oven to 200°C/
fan180°C/gas 6. Grease and line
a baking tray with baking paper.
2. Put the grated marzipan, cream
cheese, icing sugar, vanilla and half
the egg in a food processor and whizz
until smooth.
3. On a lightly floured surface, roll out
the pastry to a 3mm thick rectangle.
Fold over a 2cm strip along both the
long sides of the pastry to create a
border. Spread the apricot jam inside
the borders, then top with the marzipan
mixture. Brush the pastry edges with
the remaining beaten egg, then sprinkle
with the flaked almonds.
4. Bake for 25 minutes until the pastry is
risen and golden and the filling has set.
Cool slightly, then dust with icing sugar
and slice to serve.

## berry and apple tray bake
**Serves 6-8**
This tray bake is perfect picnic fare.

175g unsalted butter, chopped, plus
extra for greasing
300g plain flour, plus extra to dust
300ml double cream, plus extra
to serve
3 medium free-range eggs
220g caster sugar
1 tsp vanilla extract
3 green eating apples, peeled, cored,
thinly sliced and tossed with 2 tbsp
lemon juice
300g frozen mixed berries, thawed
Icing sugar to dust
Blackberry or strawberry jam to serve
(optional)

1. Preheat the oven to 180°C/
fan160°C/gas 4. Lightly grease and
flour a 32cm x 22cm baking dish.
2. In a medium pan, melt the butter
with the cream and bring to just below
boiling point over a medium heat.
Allow to cool slightly.
3. Using an electric hand mixer, beat
the eggs and sugar until pale and
fluffy. Gradually beat in the cream
mix. Sift over the flour, then fold in
with a metal spoon.
4. Stir in the vanilla, apples and mixed
berries, then pour into the prepared
dish. Bake for 40 minutes or until
golden and a skewer pushed into the
centre comes out clean.
5. Dust with icing sugar and serve
with jam and extra cream, if you like.

## festive slices
**Makes 12**

90g unsalted butter, softened, plus
extra to grease
185g brown sugar
150g plain flour, sifted
1 tsp vanilla extract
2 medium free-range eggs
2 tbsp brandy
340g mincemeat
1 tbsp self-raising flour
135g desiccated coconut
Icing sugar to dust

1. Preheat the oven to 180°C/fan160°C/
gas 4. Grease a 20cm x 30cm brownie
tin and line it with baking paper.
2. Beat the butter and 85g of the sugar
with an electric hand mixer until pale.
Stir in the plain flour and vanilla extract,
then press into the base of the tin. Bake
for 10 minutes or until pale golden.
3. Meanwhile, put the eggs in the
bowl of a stand mixer with the brandy
and the remaining 100g sugar, then
whisk until thick and pale. Stir in the
mincemeat, self-raising flour and
coconut, then spread over the base.
Bake for 25 minutes or until dark
golden, then remove from the oven
and cool slightly in the tin.
4. Turn out and cut into squares. Dust
with icing sugar and serve warm or cold.

Sultana
tray bake

## sultana tray bake
**Makes 24**

250g unsalted butter, chopped, plus
extra to grease
450g sultanas
300ml orange juice
3 medium free-range eggs
350g brown sugar
2 tsp vanilla extract
350g self-raising flour, sifted
1 tsp baking powder
Icing sugar to dust

1. Preheat the oven to 160°C/fan140°C/
gas 3. Grease a 30cm x 20cm baking
tray with butter and line the base with
baking paper.

2. Put the sultanas in a pan and cover
with the orange juice. Bring to the boil
over a medium-high heat, then reduce
the heat to medium and simmer for 15
minutes or until nearly all the juice has
been absorbed. Add the butter and stir
gently over a low heat until melted. Take
off the heat and leave to cool slightly.
3. Mix the eggs, sugar and vanilla in a
large mixing bowl. Add the flour, baking
powder and cooled sultanas, then mix
well. Pour into the lined tray and bake
for 1 hour or until firm to the touch.
(Check after 40 minutes and cover with
baking paper if it browns too quickly.)
4. Cool in the tray for 5 minutes, then
dust with icing sugar. Slice into
24 squares and serve.

## walnut brownies
**Makes 16**

200g good-quality dark chocolate (70%
cocoa solids), chopped
250g unsalted butter, chopped
300g caster sugar
4 large free-range eggs
35g cocoa powder, plus extra to dust
175g plain flour, sifted
¼ tsp baking powder
50g toasted walnuts, roughly chopped

1. Preheat the oven to 160°C/fan140°C/
gas 3. Line a 20cm square cake tin with
baking paper.
2. Put the dark chocolate and butter
in a pan over a low heat and stir until
melted. Transfer to a bowl to cool slightly.
3. Stir through the sugar, then beat in
the eggs, one at a time (don't worry if
the mixture curdles – it will come back
together). Stir in the cocoa, flour, baking
powder and a good pinch of salt, then
fold in the walnuts and pour into the tin.
4. Bake for 30-40 minutes until a skewer
pushed into the middle comes out with
only a few crumbs. Allow to cool in the
tin for 10 minutes, then transfer to
a wire rack to cool completely. Cut into
squares, dust with cocoa and serve.

Walnut brownies

Raspberry streusel slices

**Ginger and almond slices**

## raspberry streusel slices
**Serves 6-8**

150g unsalted butter, softened, plus
extra for greasing
150g ground almonds
150g caster sugar
150g self-raising flour
2 tsp cinnamon
1 medium free-range egg
160g raspberry jam
250g raspberries
Icing sugar and single cream to serve

1. Preheat the oven to 180°C/fan160°C/
gas 4. Grease a 12cm x 35cm rectangular,
fluted loose-bottomed tart tin.
2. Put the ground almonds, butter,
sugar, flour, cinnamon and egg in
a food processor and pulse until the
mixture comes together. Wrap half
the mixture in cling film and put
in the freezer for 30 minutes.
3. Press the remaining mixture into
the base and sides of the tart tin.
4. Spread the raspberry jam over the
dough and scatter raspberries over
the top. Grate over the chilled mixture
using the large holes of a box grater.
Bake for 40 minutes or until golden
(cover loosely with foil if the tart is
browning too quickly).
5. Allow to cool in the tin for 5 minutes
before turning out onto a wire rack to
cool completely. Dust with icing sugar
and serve with cream.

## ginger and almond slices
**Makes 16**

175g unsalted butter, softened, plus
extra for greasing
220g caster sugar
1 medium free-range egg
225g plain flour, sifted
2 tbsp milk
100g ground almonds
1 tsp ground ginger
125g crystallised ginger, chopped
70g flaked almonds
Icing sugar to dust
Chrysanthemum or jasmine tea
to serve (optional)

1. Preheat the oven to 190°C/fan170°C/
gas 5. Grease an 18cm x 28cm baking
tray and line it with baking paper.
2. Beat the butter and sugar using an
electric hand mixer until pale and fluffy.
Beat in the egg, then beat in the flour in
2 batches, alternating with tablespoons
of milk. Stir in the ground almonds and
all the ginger, then pat the mix into the
tin and sprinkle with the flaked almonds.
3. Bake for 35 minutes or until golden
and a skewer pushed into the centre
comes out clean.
4. Cool slightly, then transfer to a rack
to cool completely. Cut into fingers, dust
with icing sugar and serve with tea.

Strawberry and
almond tray bake

## muesli slices
**Makes 12**

100g unsalted butter, softened, plus
extra to grease
110g caster sugar
1 tsp vanilla extract
2 medium free-range eggs
45g rolled oats
100g plain flour
½ tsp baking powder
35g desiccated coconut
75g dried cherries, chopped
125g dried apricots, finely chopped
80g milk chocolate, coarsely chopped

1. Preheat the oven to 180°C/fan160°C/
gas 4. Grease a 20cm x 30cm brownie
tin or baking tin and line the base and
sides with baking paper.
2. Put the butter and sugar in the
bowl of a stand mixer and beat for
5 minutes or until pale and fluffy. Add
the vanilla extract and eggs, one at
a time, beating well after each addition.
Fold in the oats, flour and baking
powder until well combined, then fold
in the remaining ingredients.
3. Spread in an even layer in the tin,
then bake for 25-30 minutes until
golden and cooked through. Cool
completely in the tin, then cut into
12 squares and serve.

## strawberry and almond tray bake
**Makes 12**

80g chilled unsalted butter, chopped,
plus extra to grease
300g self-raising flour
3 medium free-range eggs, separated
100ml milk
185g caster sugar
240g strawberry jam
60g ground almonds
Flaked almonds to sprinkle

1. Preheat the oven to 180°C/fan160°C/
gas 4. Grease the base and sides of a
20cm x 30cm baking tin or brownie
tin and line with baking paper.
2. Put the self-raising flour, butter,
egg yolks, milk and 75g of the sugar
in a food processor. Whizz until the
mixture just comes together. Put in
the tin and, using damp hands, press
down into an even, compact layer.
3. Spread the strawberry jam evenly
over the top. In a clean bowl, whisk the
egg whites to soft peaks. Fold in the
ground almonds and the remaining
110g sugar. Spread over the jam and
scatter with the flaked almonds.
4. Bake for 30 minutes or until risen and
golden. Cool, then cut into 12 slices.

Muesli slices

# basics

## shortcrust pastry
**Makes enough for a 23cm tart case**

240g plain flour
120g chilled unsalted butter, chopped
3 tbsp iced water

1. Put the flour and butter in a food processor with a pinch of salt and whizz until you have fine crumbs. Add the iced water and process until the mixture comes together and forms a small ball.
2. Wrap in cling film and chill for 30 minutes or until ready to use.

## danish pastry dough
**Makes 2 large almond pastry plaits**

15g fresh yeast*, crumbled
3 tsp golden caster sugar
110ml whole milk, lukewarm
1 tsp almond extract
1 medium free-range egg, lightly beaten
125g plain flour, plus extra to dust
125g strong white bread flour
½ tsp ground cinnamon (optional)
110g unsalted butter, softened

1. Mix the yeast, 1 tsp of the sugar, 2 tbsp milk and the almond extract in a small bowl until smooth. Set aside in a warm place for 10 minutes. Add the rest of the milk and the egg, mix well and leave for 10 minutes more until the mixture bubbles.
2. Sift the flours, the remaining sugar, cinnamon and a pinch of salt into a large bowl, mix well and make a well in the centre. Gradually stir in the milk mixture until it forms a soft dough. Turn out onto a floured surface and knead for 5 minutes, dusting with more flour, until the dough is smooth and slightly springy to touch. On a lightly floured board, roll out to a 30cm x 40cm x 5mm thick rectangle. Cover with cling film and chill for 30 minutes.
3. Put the chilled dough on a lightly floured surface and cover two-thirds of the length of pastry with teaspoons of softened butter, 1cm apart. Leave a 1cm border, so the butter doesn't spill out during rolling.
4. Fold the butter-free third of the dough over the middle third, then fold the remaining, buttered third over the centre, too (like folding a letter into three to put inside an envelope). Lightly press down the open ends to seal, then chill, covered in cling film, for 15 minutes.
5. Remove the cling film and lay the dough on a floured surface with the short side towards you. Roll out the dough out away from you to about 1cm thick. You'll get a very long rectangle – don't worry as the next time you roll the dough it will be a more manageable size. As before, fold the bottom third of pastry over the middle third, then fold the top third over. Wrap in cling film and chill for 15 minutes more.
6. Repeat the rolling and folding process, but this time start the dough on the floured surface with the longest side facing you. Chill for another 15 minutes.
7. Repeat steps 5 and 6, so you've rolled the dough into a long rectangle 4 times.
8. Wrap the dough with cling film and chill overnight until firm. Trim the edges; the dough is now ready to use.

* Available from the bakery section of large supermarkets such as Sainsbury's.

## ganache

**Makes about 500g**

150g milk chocolate, chopped
150g dark chocolate, chopped
125ml double cream
50g unsalted butter

1. Fill a pan one-third full with water and bring to a gentle simmer. Put all the ingredients in a small heatproof bowl set over the pan (make sure the base of the bowl doesn't touch the water). Stir until smooth and melted. Cool slightly.

## custard

**Makes 625ml**

5 egg yolks
55g caster sugar
500ml single cream
1 vanilla pod, split, seeds scraped

1. Gently whisk the egg yolks and caster sugar in a bowl until well combined. Put the cream, vanilla pod and seeds in a pan over a medium heat and bring to just below boiling point. Pour the hot cream over the egg mixture, whisking gently to combine.
2. Return the mixture to a clean pan over a very low heat. Stir with a wooden spoon for 5-6 minutes until the mixture thickens and coats the back of the spoon – watch carefully as you don't want to scramble the eggs. (If it does curdle, put everything, except the vanilla pod, in a blender, add an ice cube and blend well. Keep your fingers crossed.)

3. Strain into a jug. Cover the surface closely with baking paper to prevent a skin forming. Serve warm or chilled.

## tomato chutney

**Makes 4-5 jars**

1.5kg red, green or semi-ripe tomatoes
400g shallots, peeled
3 tart eating apples, such as granny smith
2 red chillies
3 garlic cloves, finely chopped
Large knob of fresh ginger
550ml cider vinegar
1 tbsp white mustard seeds
400g sultanas
175g light muscovado sugar
60g black treacle

1. Roughly chop the tomatoes, then put them in a large preserving pan.
2. Chop the shallots, then peel, core and chop the apples. Add them to the pan with the tomatoes.
3. Deseed and finely dice the chillies. Grate the ginger, then add it to the pan with the chillies and chopped garlic. Pour over three-quarters of the vinegar.
4. Stir in the white mustard seeds, sultanas, sugar and treacle, then cook over a medium heat for 5-10 minutes, stirring, until the sugar has dissolved. Season, then simmer for 1 hour until very thick. Add the remaining vinegar, then remove from the heat. Spoon into sterilised jars and seal. The cooled chutney will keep in a dark, cool place for up to a year.

# tips & tricks

## getting started

Always read the recipe, then gather and prepare the ingredients, doing any chopping, sifting and the like before you begin. We generally prefer to measure by weight. For liquids, we use these measurements (use proper measuring spoons, as the teaspoons and tablespoons used for cutlery are not necessarily accurate).

1 tbsp = 15ml
1 tsp = 5ml

## essential items

• Round springform cake tins (hard-anodised aluminium is best) in sizes such as 20cm, 23cm and 25cm
• At least one brownie tin, ideally 18cm x 26cm and/or 20cm x 30cm
• Solid baking trays, preferably stainless steel, which don't buckle
• Baking sheets, flat with no sides, are ideal for baking biscuits and scones
• Keep one or two wire racks for cooling; stainless steel is best
• Non-stick baking paper to line tins
• A piping bag for decorating (or use a zip-lock bag with a corner cut off)

## preparing tins

• To line a round cake tin, put on baking paper and trace around using a pencil. Cut out a circle for the base. Cut out a strip of paper long enough to line the side of the tin. Grease the tin with butter, then put the paper inside and smooth with your hands to fit.
• To line a baking tray or brownie tin, cut a rectangular sheet of baking paper to fit the base of the tin with plenty overhanging two of the sides – this will make it easier to lift the cake from the tin. Grease the tin and line with the paper, smoothing it with your hands to fit.

# index

# SUBSCRIBE TODAY

to the UK's best food magazine and we'll send you a set of Salter digital kitchen scales worth £39.99, absolutely FREE.

## GREAT REASONS TO SUBSCRIBE

- You'll never miss an issue of **delicious.** with convenient home delivery every month
- Receive a FREE set of compact Salter kitchen scales worth £39.99
- Fantastic savings – save up to 34% on the full subscription price
- Pay as little as £29.99 for 12 issues

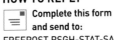

☎ **0844 848 8419**
(please quote DMBS0912)

---

## Free Salter kitchen scales

☑ **YES!** I would like to take advantage of the exclusive subscription offer I've ticked below...

☐ **DIRECT DEBIT OFFER** £29.99 every 12 issues (SAVE OVER 34%) + FREE Salter kitchen scales

☐ **CHEQUE OR CREDIT CARD OFFER** £33.99 for 12 issues (SAVE 25%) + FREE Salter kitchen scales

This subscription is: ☐ For me   ☐ A gift

**YOUR DETAILS** (essential) Mr/Mrs/Ms/Miss

Forename _____ Surname _____

Address _____

Postcode _____ Email _____

Daytime phone _____ Mobile phone _____

**GIFT RECIPIENT'S DETAILS** If giving **delicious.** as a gift, please ensure you complete the recipient's details (below) and your own details (above).

Mr/Mrs/Ms/Miss _____ Forename _____

Surname _____

Address _____

Postcode _____

**COMPLETE SECTION (1)** Direct Debit **(2)** Cheque or **(3)** Credit/debit card

**(1) DIRECT DEBIT PAYMENT** £29.99 **EVERY 12 ISSUES (UK ONLY)**

Instruction to your bank or building society to pay by Direct Debit

DIRECT Debit

To the manager (bank name) _____

Branch address _____

Postcode _____

Account in the name(s) of _____

Originator's identification no

| 6 | 9 | 6 | 7 | 6 | 1 |

Ref no to be completed by delicious. magazine

Bank/building society account no
☐☐☐☐☐☐☐☐

Branch sort code
☐☐ ☐☐ ☐☐

Please pay **delicious.** magazine (part of Eye to Eye Media Ltd) Direct Debits from the account detailed in this instruction, subject to the safeguards assured by the Direct Debit Guarantee. I understand this instruction may remain with the originator and, if so, details will be passed electronically to my bank/building society.

Signature(s) _____ Date _____

Banks and building societies may not accept Direct Debit instructions for some types of account.

**(2)** ☐ I enclose a cheque for £33.99 made payable to **delicious.** magazine

**(3)** Please charge £33.99 to my:

Visa ☐   MasterCard ☐   Maestro ☐ (issue no ☐☐)   Maestro only

Card number ☐☐☐☐ ☐☐☐☐ ☐☐☐☐ ☐☐☐☐

Valid from ☐☐ ☐☐   Expiry date ☐☐ ☐☐

Signature(s) _____ Date _____

### HOW TO REPLY

📧 **Complete this form and send to:**
FREEPOST RSGH-STAT-SASB
delicious. magazine
Sittingbourne ME9 8GU
(NO STAMP REQUIRED)

📞 **0844 848 8419**
(please quote DMBS0912)

 delicious.subscribeonline.co.uk
(please quote DMBS0912)

DMBS0912

# delicious.

EYE TO EYE MEDIA LTD, AXE & BOTTLE COURT,
70 NEWCOMEN STREET, LONDON SE1 1YT

Editor **Karen Barnes**
Deputy editor **Susan Low**
Editorial assistant **Sarah Simpson**
Food editor **Lizzie Kamenetzky**
Deputy food editor **Rebecca Smith**
Cookery assistant **Charlie Clapp**
Art director **Jocelyn Bowerman**
Art editor **Martine Tinney**
Chief sub editor **Les Dunn**
Deputy chief sub editor **Hugh Thompson**
Sub editor **Rebecca Almond**
Promotions and web manager **Becca Bailey**
With thanks to **Felicity Cloake, Hannah Thompson**

Managing director **Seamus Geoghegan**
Publisher **Adrienne Moyce**
Consultant editorial director **Jo Sandilands**
Circulation director **Owen Arnot**
Production manager **Jake Hopkins**

**Editorial enquiries** 020 7803 4100, readers@deliciousmagazine.co.uk
**Magazine subscription enquiries** 0844 848 8419
**Web** deliciousmagazine.co.uk

### Recipes
**delicious.** food team, Olivia Andrews, Felicity Barnum-Bobb, Kate Bishop, Jessica Brook, Jill Dupleix, Carla Egar, Amanda Grant, Cherie Hausler, Belinda Jeffery, Valli Little, Debbie Major, Kate Nichols, Tom Norrington-Davies, Jacqueline Pietrowski, Trudelies Schouten, Kylie Walker, Lucy Williams, Phoebe Wood, Hannah Yeadon

### Photographs
Steve Brown, Peter Cassidy, Ben Dearnley, Tara Fisher, Jonathan Gregson, TASTE/Denver Hendricks/lifestylefeatures.com, TASTE/Stephen Inggs/lifestylefeatures.com, Dan Jones, Mowie Kay, David Loftus, Mark O'Meara, Lis Parsons, TASTE/Dirk Pieters/lifestylefeatures.com, TASTE/Shane Powell/lifestylefeatures.com, Claire Richardson, Craig Robertson, Mark Roper, Jeremy Simons, Maja Smend, Brett Stevens, Studio Philippi, Peter Thiedeke, Karen Thomas, Eric van Lokven, TASTE/Dawie Verwey/South Africa/lifestylefeatures.com, Ian Wallace, Philip Webb, Stuart West, Kate Whitaker, Rob White

### Styling
Karen Akhtar, Liz Belton, Julz Beresford, Phillippa Cheifitz, Yael Grinham, Jane Hann, Lisa Harrison, Rachel Jukes, Alice Lindley, Hilary Lowe, Lucy McKelvie, Rob Merrett, David Morgan, Michelle Noerianto, Louise Pickford, Studio Philippi, Polly Webb-Wilson, Helen Webster, Jan Willem van Reik, Kristen Wilson